# MY HUCKLEBERRY'S RESCUE JOURNEY

## Horse Connections Through Quantum Entanglement

ANNA GASSIB

# DEDICATION

This book is dedicated to my wonderful family, my barn family, and the countless horses that have been by my side throughout this journey.

# ABOUT THE AUTHOR

## ANNA GASSIB, MA, Licensed Counselor

## Entrepreneur, Equestrian and Empowering Spirit

Anna Gassib is a Licensed Counselor, earning her Master's degree in Applied Psychology and Mental Health Counseling from NYU. She is also certified in DBT, Gestalt coaching and personal coaching. Her expertise in these fields makes her uniquely qualified to guide individuals and groups through any life challenges.

Gassib worked many years as a senior executive at leading financial institutions in the US. Gassib along with others established A Women's Entrepreneurial Group. In the spirit of entrepreneurialism, Gassib started her own business with a single pony in her backyard in 2004. Since then, has transformed into a successful equestrian center with two-fold missions to help build small businesses That focuses on the horse and human connections and to improve the quality of life for individuals in need of therapeutic intervention.

Gassib, traded her high-profile career in finance at large banking institutions forr an entrepreneurial opportunity that combined her love of horses with her commitment to help others. After many years of acquiring struggling stables and making them profitable again, Gassib turned her attention to helping others. Most recently, she assumed what was a defunct facility in New Jersey and turned it into a profitable business in just one year. At this facility she established a nonprofit and designed a program that combines her skills as a Licensed Therapist and a Life coach to empower men, women and children who are trying to find the correct path for their lives. The stables are now home to more than 70 horses that provide a variety of services to help their human partners.

Among the people served by the program are individuals struggling with addiction, children with special needs, behavioral issues, families who cope with mental illness and veterans who suffer from post-traumatic stress disorder. Gassib has partnered with many organizations throughout the local area and hopes to expand the program across the East coast. Equine therapy has long been recognized as a meaningful and long-term approach to a variety of mental health and medical issues and has been known to "heal the soul," an outcome close to Gassib's heart.

# CONTENTS

# I

# The Assignment

Equine therapy and how it enhances our relationship with ourselves and our surroundings has been an area of interest for countless philosophers throughout history. A renowned political leader, Abraham Lincoln, said, "*I can make a General in five minutes, but a good horse is hard to replace.*"
Horses are generally seen as the epitome of balance and companionship. Throughout history, equine therapy has been known to improve cognitive processes also known as thinking and emotional well-being. These highly loyal animals make great human companions as they help us understand the world that exists beyond the physical structures of reality and lies within abstract values.

Displaying immense admiration and respect for these four-legged companions, Isabella, an ambitious woman with well-versed academic qualifications and a licensed psychotherapist with a degree from a well-respected university, left behind her corporate job to focus on her venture, a multimillion-dollar equestrian facility. She had a niche interest in equine therapy and the contribution horses make to improving human connection, internally and externally.

Isabella's findings about horses are based on her work and intuition regarding horses. She didn't want to stand isolated with her interpretations of horses, so she was set on a quest to find programs to support her in learning more about them. Isabella's daughters, like their mother, inherited their mom's passion for horses. They experienced the incredible impact horses have on people throughout their lives. Through showing their horses, they visited many equestrian facilities along the East Coast of the United States.

Regardless of Isabella's excellence in her work, she stayed in tune with her emotional and spiritual self. She observed life beyond the typical lens and had the drive to dig deeper into the meanings and intricate details to build a connection with herself, the surroundings, and the greater good.

She had a habit of letting her logical brain drive her career decisions, but she did not neglect her conscience in pursuit of being successful. Isabella has had her fair share of complications in her life; when she was twelve, she lost her mother. She belonged to a lower-middle-class family, lived with her single father, and witnessed her father struggle to pay the bills and have a solid financial standing, even though he worked full-time alongside additional part-time shifts. Despite this, Isabella has a flattering approach to life and prefers to view the world through an encouraging lens. Isabella refuses to let her past trauma hinder her accomplishments and likes to live in the moment. Isabella understood pain and suffering to be crucial to human existence, and instead of turning cruel in the face of adversity, she challenged herself to be empathetic and strong-willed.

She was able to make her financial breakthrough before turning thirty. Currently, her focus is on her facility, which operates with the exploration of the relationship between humans and horses and how it can help us grow spiritually and mentally. Given her interest in therapy and her search for a program that promoted equine therapy to enhance our connection within our spiritual and emotional selves, she met Melinda, who seemed like Isabella's twin flame.

Melinda, a retired cop from New England, has also encountered tremendous traumatic situations. Originating from a broken family with alcoholic parents, she was abandoned by her mother while her father was psychologically and physically abusive to her. She left her abusive home as soon as she turned legal. But she got trapped with an abusive husband., who she divorced, displaying much courage.

Sharing her love for horses with Isabella, even Melinda wished to dedicate her life and work to studying and being around these majestic animals. Regardless of her unstable past life, Melinda refused to relinquish herself to her problems; she never let her setbacks define the person she was. She continued to carry hope for a better life while raising three daughters on her own. Committed to serving others with integrity and compassion, Melinda firmly believes in human connections and the meaning they add to life. She tries to find the best in everyone and everything, even in the darkest moments.

Both these women shared similar perceptions towards life. They are lively and outgoing, with a charming physique and healthy lifestyles. They like to travel and live without drastic evaluations while remaining grounded in their values and morals. They both pull strength from their trials and tribulations, and find comfort in the knowledge that the sun will rise each morning even if they can not see it.

The first time Isabella and Melinda met was during the first meeting from the program they both had opted for, where they were assigned each other as partners and were required to converse for 30 days over calls. The assignment was that the other would stay silent while one person was speaking. Without hindering the talk, they would only listen and not react. This proved to be a challenging exercise, as both of them were outgoing. Isabella and Melinda decided to speak at 08:00 P.M. when they would get done with work and other commitments to attend to this task with their undivided attention. Initially, the aim of the task appeared ambiguous and vague, but it started becoming clear by the time of the third call. The call's content wasn't limited to boundaries; they could speak about their day, emotions, or something bothering them.

During the first meeting, they instantly connected over shared world views and their unique experience-driven interest in equine therapy. "*The plant of success is rooted in the seeds of misery; without pain, the mere purpose of life would be limited to birth and death. Pain is what makes the middle part more exciting.*" Melinda smirked, referring to Isabella.

"*I agree; the adversity in life brings us closer to the mystics. The tenderness in the pain of a loved one is a bittersweet feeling that seems horrifying but gives birth to philosophies, poetries, and art. Without pain, healing wouldn't exist. And without healing, art wouldn't exist.*" Isabella added.

One could tell how humbled these two women looked upon meeting each other; they felt as if they were a direct reflection of each other's virtues. They spoke to each other for a while before leaving. They talked to each other during the first session without realizing the time. Both of them were overwhelmed by meeting each other. After hours of shared laughter, empowering conversations, and deciding arrangements for the scheduled call, Isabella and Melinda waved goodbye to each other.

Apart from their united ethical and moral norms, the girls exceptionally bonded over their shared love for horses, and their characters reflected nuances similar to the horses. They were spiritually acclaimed throughout their lives, so their connection with horses relied on a scientific principle in accordance with the notions of spirituality.

While returning from a meeting with Melinda, Isabella had a rare, subtle smile that day. During the entire car ride, she thought about her interaction with Melinda. It was too good to be accurate. Her feelings were similar to Melinda's; she was equally delighted to have met Isabella that day.

After speaking with Isabella, Melinda was lost in her thoughts on her way back. An interesting scientific phenomenon that linked physics with human relationships occurred to her mind as she recalled Quantum entanglement, a scientific theory rooted in the study of quantum mechanics. It states that some particles, despite their physical location, remain interdependent through entanglement. This concept is related to the spiritual perception of the interconnectivity between humans. She couldn't help but smile when she realized that meeting Isabella brought to life the thoughts and principles she had read in books and on the internet. Both Isabella and Melinda were spiritually opinionated and had profound knowledge about the implications of faith. Initially, they belonged to broken homes, but their passion for turning pain into power brought them close together.

Their calls and meetings proved that they both were intrigued by studying and observing horses' behaviors because both excelled at regulating their emotions. All their life, Isabella and Melinda had managed to find meaning in very little. Instead of blaming their surroundings, they used the harshness of life as a motivator to contribute to a better world. Their purpose revolved around serving humanity and animals, particularly horses. By comprehending the cognitive process in horses, they found a reason for staying alive, which was far more than surviving. And perhaps their longing for a world that is above a physical sense manifested the connection that mirrored their essence of being. Although they met coincidentally, Isabella and Melinda were unaware of the change this event was to bring into their lives.

# II

# A Shift in Perspective

Belief is powerful; it isn't just the idea of a belief but the overall system that makes it valid. The more you dig into an idea to explore it, stronger your belief becomes, and the more you wish to stay on the path. It is because it adds value to your existence. Your beliefs define your purpose, and the purpose defines your essence. We, humans, are nothing without our ability to develop faith in an entity or simply a notion. That said, beliefs go beyond the notions of physical requirements or reasoning.

Some legends gave birth to the idea of a soul train, according to which, when an ambulance is stopped by a passing train, it means that the person in the ambulance isn't meant to live and will pass away shortly. This is just one story, but you would be shocked to hear the kinds of tales that stay true for quite a few people. Different cultures have developed their versions of stories that seem to resonate with them.

The question is, why do humans make stories of this sort? Is it to create mass confusion, or is it mere human nature? Well, the answer is quite simple if you ponder over it, and it has already been said above: it is to add a sense of

purpose to life. Each individual's tendency to live for and by a purpose varies, but the absence of purpose means a body without a soul

## Horse Connections through Quantum Entanglement

When we talk about having a purpose, Isabella and Melinda's lives represent the pursuit of a passion that fuels their very essence. In addition, both of these women found each other through coincidence to grow into a shared purpose for meaning—their admiration for horses. The project that Isabella and Melinda were assigned came off as unclear at first, but gradually, it started making sense to them. The more they talked, the more they felt inclined towards a shared purpose. Their perception of life was aligned with each other.

To think of it, how miraculous is it to find such connections that don't demand anything from you? They don't have an intent to drain anything from you, and if anything, they don't expect much. They are there for the sole reason of bringing happiness into your life. Their love feels unconditional, and these are the bonds that you want to nurture.

"Melinda, at first, the nature of this project was quite ambiguous to me, but gradually, I have been able to grasp the meaning behind the task. You know, sometimes silence can be uncomfortable, especially when we are young and our brains are developing." Isabella said to Melinda.

Melinda smiled indistinctly and said, "You're right, Isabella. The landscape of this world has changed significantly over the past few decades. With these advanced technology tools and the prevailing use of social media, our minds find it difficult to ground themselves at the moment. I hope I don't sound like an old grandma who hates mobile phones because I don't; if anything, modern technology has made our lives a lot easier. All I mean is that we need to sustain the balance between real connections and unrealistic social media standards."

Isabella chuckled at Melinda's grandma's comment and said, "Yes, I understand your point. It's not the development of social media that's harmful; it's rather about the control we hand over to our devices. We need to know that the phones are not supposed to control us; we should be able to control them."

Melinda nodded, approving Isabella's remark.

Intelligence is often perceived as conditional to one's ability to learn and memorize a specific subject quickly. However, intelligence can be subjective and have various forms. Other than the typical perception of intelligence, an aspect of intelligence is directed at the ability to regulate one's emotions by observing the surroundings. That said, significant observations are rooted in being able to listen to others with an open mind. Over the past few decades, our world has witnessed a shift in digitalization. It is a long debate to conclude whether content creation and consumption have added or reduced value from our relationships. However, one thing that we can agree on is that valuing a stronger internet connection does not necessarily mean greater connectivity. In a world ruled by memes and reels, it is important to find time to focus on the present moments with the ones we cherish the most.

Horses have an innate ability to perceive others' emotions. That happens because they're harmonized with their surroundings; they can pick up on the clues of the energy that prevails to know the deceitful lies humans tell. Not only that, but they also know when someone is lying to themselves—that's formidable. These majestic animals have such mysteriously fascinating traits that never fail to amaze you. Listening to others' opinions with an active mind is particularly important because the insights you gain by doing so are invaluable. Sometimes, we underestimate the underlying value of it until we are forcibly made to sit with our thoughts, which we then find scary.

That is what happened with Isabella and Melinda. They couldn't realize the importance of attentiveness until they took the time to understand the nature of the task, which was to enhance listening. There isn't a cheat code for some abstract concepts of life, but when you observe life through someone else's lens, you find unique perspectives to understand your problems. During their calls, Isabella and Melinda found themselves transitioning – in a good way. The ability to listen to someone else's life is not mainly an easy thing to do. Still, through this assignment, Isabella and Melinda found themselves going from wanting to express themselves to genuinely listening to each other's challenges. It helped them open their mind, and they started witnessing that hearing the other person brought them closer to themselves; they were able to find solutions to their own hurdles.

The hustles we involve ourselves throughout the week make us crave connections that are uplifting for the soul. The purpose of life seems meaningless without the bonds we have around us. The volatile nature of life is that many come and leave, but some stay in the heart forever. Some people instantly make a home in our hearts. They make you feel as if you have already shared a lifetime with them. To put that unique connection in words would be underestimating its importance; however much you speak of it doesn't feel enough. Isabella and Melinda craved this all their lives: to have a friend with whom they could find resonance and express their true selves. Now, finally, they had each other. Their bond was a special one because it was as if they heard the melody of each other's soul. Although they had different lives, their challenges and interests were similar.

Isabella and Melinda were both strong women with profound character; their natures radiated high frequencies. Both of them were fulfilled and secure within themselves and sought people around them who would genuinely add value to their lives. They weren't intimidated by loneliness, which made them resilient. For these reasons, Isabella and Melinda's relationship was transforming from working together on an assignment to personally connecting over mutual experiences and interests. They talked about their love for their children and horses, discussed day-to-day activities, and indulged in constructive, philosophical arguments. When they were conversing, nothing could distract them; they were fully involved and attentive to each other.

"You know, Isabella, when I divorced my husband, people around me would empathize with my sadness, although I wasn't really sad. The divorce meant freedom for me because I wasn't happy with him. I do understand that their advice was coming from a place of care. However, it makes me wonder why the vast majority consider being alone as being unhappy. Well, I think nothing screams of loneliness more than living with someone who constantly misunderstands the nuances of your soul. To me, it was like being inside a monster's cage; I realized the importance of my individuality and solitude. After we separated, I decided only to let someone in when they made me feel better than my alone time. How I love spending time by myself!" Melinda said to Isabella.

Isabella smiled at her new best friend and said, "I understand your point. I think it's our society that has conditioned us to believe that happiness comes through a romantic relationship. I mean, it's not that romantic relationships can't make you happy; they're a part of your life. There are many people in this world who are in relationships; does that necessarily mean they're happy? I don't think so. If you ask me about happiness, I think it comes from embracing your unique sense of individuality. I think the singular meaning of life is to get closer to yourself every day; that's what brings me happiness."

"I also think that we spend a lot of time chasing happiness without really understanding the essence of it. I don't think happiness is a state of achievement. It's a transitory state of consciousness. And in the end, what's light without the dark, right? How do we realize happiness in the absence of sadness?" Melinda said.

"Wow! Transitory state of consciousness? You're so smart, honestly, Melinda. God, I think I need to write that down. And you're absolutely right; we try to objectify happiness, give labels to it, but it's rather subjective."

Isabella and Melinda were as well-spoken as they were brilliant. Their soft natures reflected their kind hearts. They loved to talk to each other; for them, it was an unofficial therapy session. Their intuitive abilities were aligned at each other's level, and this is a significant reason why they connected with each other on an intimate level.

Language is an integral part of human life. However, the third eye, or intuition, does not require a language to convey its message. Intuition is well-known as a natural ability granted to humans at birth. This feeling can be learned and implemented. Intuition acts in the decision-making process concerning our past experiences. A classic study is explained by Elaine Fox in her book Switch Craft to understand intuition. The participants had to choose cards from two decks. Unknowingly, the researchers rigged the decks, with one resulting in huge victories and massive losses, while the other one's outcome was small gains and small losses. After ten rounds, the participants were able to figure out the dangerous deck. Interestingly, the researchers noticed increased hot flashes among the participants when choosing the risky deck. Consequently, the researchers reached a conclusion portraying an intuitive bias when the participants selected the cards. This confirms the claim that intuitive abilities are a gameplay of the unconscious mind. This study also implies that recognizing instincts can lead to greater intuitive understanding. Learning to hear the voice that rests inside every human can help one to master the craft of using intuition as a guide. This ability is immensely found in horses. They do not know how to speak a language but know when humans lie, even to themselves.

This would be the sort of discussion that Isabella and Melinda would usually have. They could talk about it day and night without getting tired. They made arguments that were aligned with both scientific and spiritual concepts.

"You know, Isabella, I've heard claims from some scientists justifying the absence of God in this universe. As far as my understanding of science is concerned, I believe the more I delve into scientific theories, the more I see the relationship between spirituality and science. Just consider the concept of the infinite universe; we have reached so far in advancements, but no scientist has yet claimed that we have explored the entire universe. In fact, they say the opposite; we haven't even witnessed it partially. When you study God, his abilities also seem infinite; it goes beyond human imagination and the seven skies. For this reason, I don't see the disconnection between science and religion; they can co-exist." Isabella said to Melinda.

Melinda replied, "You're right, and I feel the same. There could be only so many nights when I would run my mind over this. I think it's important to maintain the balance between reality and spirituality. My uncle once told me that true knowledge lies in knowing mathematics but being grounded enough to perceive the power of mystics."

The calls between Isabella and Melinda were not just for its sake now; they were moving on to the next level of their friendship. Gradually, their bond was transitioning into something more profound and personal. Both of them shared an immaculate connection in each other's presence. They lived for the same ambition, which was to serve humanity. Melinda left her career as a police officer behind in retaliation to her divorce from her husband, who worked in the police – she couldn't stand the sight of her past intervening with her present. Isabella had her own baggage of a dysfunctional family, but similar to Melinda, she did not use her trauma to escape reality. Melinda now worked to make equine therapy accessible to all, along with Isabella, who was as enthusiastic about the idea of working with horses to improve the quality of their own and others' lives. The shift in perspective that the ladies experienced was, in reality, a kick-start to a companionship that they had always longed for - Isabella and Melinda were destined to meet each other to fulfill their calling.

# III

# A Weekend Revelation

*"The best way to predict the future is to create it."* – Peter Ducker.

When you consider it, the validity of this quote hits you like a brick. We humans often let our past mistakes or circumstances dictate our present and future. If you weigh it on a scale, you are damaging the integrity of both your present and future—a future that could have otherwise been better only if your focus was dedicated to the present. In a world that heavily relies on digital communication mediums, distractions are inevitable, and staying grounded in the current instants is rendered unimportant. However, as humans, it is our right to find the mindset to keep ourselves away from events that hold no meaning to our present reality.

One purpose of Isabella and Melinda's calls was to help them stay in the present moment without worrying about the unfortunate events of the past and let go of future worries. This was the shift in perspective that we talked about in the last part. However, Isabella and Melinda's journey had some surprises for them – something that would bring them closer to each other, the values of general life, and horses. Both of them understood that in order to welcome a positive change, sometimes life throws bricks at you that may seem painful at the moment. However, they also understood that without pain, there is no power. At last, a diamond is a piece of coal that refuses to give up. When we talk about humans, we are far more resilient than an object. Imagine the diamond souls and minds we would have if, instead of resisting the pain, we embraced its power.

After the busy week, the weekend was approaching, which meant it was time for Isabella and Melinda to see each other face to face. The following weekend was supposed to be their coaching weekend. This was the next step in Isabella and Melinda's careers. After weeks of gaining insights through calls with each other, Isabella and Melinda's project offered them an experience equivalent to clinical work. Their calls would continue, but their journey with clinical work would take them to the next level. To their delight, Isabella and Melinda were in the same group. Both women were excited to work with each other on the project they loved. Talking through calls was itself comforting for them, but meeting each other was a different experience. The bond they shared was becoming more personal now that they had met.

Human psychology is a complicated discipline. Over time, we have witnessed multiple psychological health issues surface. Consequently, we have also noticed the emergence of various psychologists. But can we say that every mental health practitioner or coach is the best at their duties? Out of every field, psychology is the one that does not only require textbook nerds and experienced professors with little implementation of empathy and emotional regulation capabilities. Being a psychologist means helping individuals navigate their life patterns in a way that leads to their betterment. If one isn't passionate about helping others, the whole meaning of this profession falls apart. Gladly, Isabella and Melinda did not opt for this profession out of any other purpose but for others' improvement – to help them understand the meaning of life and extract their purpose from it. Just as Isabella and Melinda overcame their obstacles to allow brilliant perspectives to flow, they wanted the same for everyone. They understood the profession to a level where they knew that without being able to empathize with others' feelings and experiences, they could not help them. Their intents were pure, and their actions were practically oriented. They were never negligent in their work duties, and their steadfast commitment makes the two of them unique.

Isabella and Melinda worked with clients and students to understand the implications of mental health. They gathered data from real-world patients to help with mental health interventions. During the first coaching weekend, they started chatting about their daughters, whom they loved very much. As usual, their conversation revolved around their deep love for their daughters and horses.

Isabella looked at Melinda and said, "Melinda, isn't it a great topic to wonder how much horses teach us about synchronization and the oneness of humans? To think of it, all of us have different matter but carry the same energy. We take birth in this world, free of impurities or judgment. Only when we grow up do we find ourselves immersed in human patterns: the flaws and imperfections. We fail to perceive that while our forms may differ, our essence is the same. We all breathe the same air and live under the same sky."

Melinda replied, "Yeah, and that principle can easily be grasped by riding a horse. You know, in order to ride one, how we need to make sure that the horse's spine is relieved of any stress or pressure. When riding one, we need to make sure that we are not exerting any downward pressure on a horse's back. Their spine is connected to the nervous system, a part of the brain responsible for controlling the body's actions. To apply force on a horse's back would be applying pressure on their nervous system."

During a ride, the movements of the horse and its rider are dictated by the laws of physics. A study conducted to comprehend Riders' Effects on Horses helps us understand the biomechanical laws that take place between the horse and the rider.[1] One cannot indulge in equestrian sports unless one understands the physical laws involved. The very notions of horse riding, which seem intriguing, drew Isabella and Melinda's attention towards them. Through learning about horses, they were able to connect with the elements of nature.

---

[1] https://www.ncbi.nlm.nih.gov/pmc/articles/PMC10741103/

The more they devoted themselves to the equestrian way of life, the more they understood humanity in the larger picture.

Another exciting aspect of horses' effects is that they help us with our cognitive patterns. Although this area still requires the attention of multiple research and development experts, the existing research indicates positive mental health impacts of horse interactions. Horses have an optimistic impact on our mental and spiritual well-being: they boost self-awareness, encourage mindfulness, ease stress, and help us with the decision-making process. A study conducted at the University of Mississippi unveils the psychological health benefits horses add to our lives.[2] These were the underlying reasons for Isabella and Melinda's attraction towards these sublime creatures of nature.

During a conversation, Melinda told Isabella about her daughter's passion for rescuing and nurturing horses. Melinda's daughter, Cassie, had witnessed the adversities of a broken home. Being raised in a violent home impacts children, making Cassie a sensitive little girl. She channels her pain by rescuing several animals and providing them with a safe shelter. That added purpose to Cassie's life, just like her mother. When one observes uncertainty and confusion in the family dynamic, it is normal for them to show vulnerability towards change. Cassie had experienced the ambiguity in her father's love for her. When her father was violent toward her mother, she would take the stand. However, as a child, she craved her father's love during other times. Cassie's circumstances made her internalize the pain to a level where she struggles to be vocal about her boundaries and faces issues such as low self-esteem. Melinda was aware of her daughter's struggles, so she provided her with a safe space. Melinda was no alien to the psychological impacts of a broken home, and she made sure to make her daughter's mental health a priority. Cassie had purchased

---

2

https://archives.joe.org/joe/2019june/rb6.php#:~:text=Results%20suggest%20that%20interaction%20with,Implications%20exist%20for%20Extension%20programming.

a horse to rescue and was waiting for its arrival. However, her frustration grew when the delivery was delayed, and so did Melinda's.

After their coaching weekend on Sunday, Melinda and Isabella were ready to part ways to head home. The women decided that they would resume their calls the following Tuesday. Isabella's seven-hour drive home was particularly exhausting, and she couldn't feel her limbs just after a few hours. However, being an optimist, Isabella knew that complaining about little things wouldn't bring her satisfaction as much as practicing gratitude would. Fatigued from the day's activities, Isabella put on a couple of motivating channels to listen to. Soon after, she was feeling calm. Isabella was reminiscing about the day she had with Melinda.

Change seems far-fetched to us at times. When we look at progress through surface-level meaning, it appears as though it isn't worth the chase. Nevertheless, change in the broader perspective is worth consideration: the change that comes through a mindset. The interactions between Isabella and Melinda did not contribute as much to their material success as much as it did to their emotional one. The two women were already successful in their worldly encounters, but their life's goal wasn't limited to it. They sought the meaning that comes through beliefs, reasoning, humility, and balance. They knew that monetary success serves restrictive goals in life, but intellectual and spiritual success serves an everlasting purpose. It adds contentment to life and makes one capable of living for the right moments. Without pining over the causes or the outcomes of behavior, Isabella and Melinda bowed down to the compassion that the present moment held, for it may never come again. These thoughts were central to Isabella's life, and of course, her new best friend, Melinda, mirrored hers.

Isabella reflected on the person she had become over the course of time. She thought of her journey, its good and bad parts. She circled about the results of human evolution and decided that in order to become the best version of yourself, you need to accept the changes that life brings.

Horse Connections through Quantum Entanglement

A few hours into the ride, Isabella found herself deep in the pits of her mind, thinking about life, "I don't wish for a time in life when my thoughts would stop evolving; it is the process of transformation that has made me who I am. However, the past was, would I be in the same mind if those things didn't happen? The time we spend to control the future results, do we realize that each moment spent is a lost second to the future, something that hasn't occurred yet? Would my worry about the future have a positive impact on it, or would it just mean for me to lose the luxury of the very moments? The freedom to live for the right instants is non-negotiable. Instead of focusing on a defined beginning or an end, I should be thinking about the incredible journey I have traveled. When I take the last few breaths, instead of feeling regretful about losing time, I want to thank this little life that leveraged its incredible wisdom for me."

Being around horses, Isabella experienced significant growth in her perception. She saw life through a lens that she had not before. Matters of intuition started becoming apparent to her, and she understood energy levels differently. Isabella was drawn more toward the deep meanings of notions instead of seeking temporary solutions. Her work with horses, combined with her best friend's arrival in her life, made her appreciate the current moments. Although she was a natural at attributing empathy, somehow, being close to horses weighed on her awareness. She could interpret the values of humanity in the truest sense. She was able to acknowledge the fact that everyone has their own baggage. In the light of your own problems, it is cruel if you disregard other people's suffering. Isabella knew that no matter how different humans appear on the outside, we are made of the same biological molecules. Our problems are connected with each other's in ways that we cannot imagine. Only companionship can help each of us come out of our problems. Every person that you meet is a manifestation of your personal beliefs. At least, this was Isabella and Melinda's case.

The Sunday weekend proved hectic for Isabella because of the tiring drive.

The week went by with the usual activities. Isabella and Melinda were occupied with business, but Melinda had something going on in her mind. Cassie's horse hadn't arrived yet, and it seemed to worry her daughter. Melinda was concerned about its arrival and continued calling the facility but to no avail. Melinda and Isabella were utterly unaware of the events that would unfold and bring them further closer to each other. Just as they believed, the reason behind Isabella and Melinda's friendship was not going to be a mystery to them anymore. These women were set on a path of a shared experience that would leave them in dismay and surprise. This weekend revelation might bring an unexpected change in their life that they wouldn't have thought of.

# IV

# A Suspenseful Return

After Isabella's seven-hour drive, the week unfolded, filled with many happenings. Monday went by in the blink of an eye, and an extremely hectic schedule left very little space for Isabella to have time by herself. Tuesday would hopefully be different because it was the time when the ladies would resume their calls. The women had decided to suspend their calls for a while to immerse themselves in the weekend experience. This also meant some time out to reflect on the fieldwork and the coaching weekend. Although this was a professionally assigned task, for Melinda and Isabella, it served as an escape, a chance to connect with themselves. With each call, the nature of the project became more apparent to them, and they were able to immerse themselves in the heart of the experiment. Their call this week was about their achievements and the way that led them to it.

For Isabella, it was her belief in her dreams. Everything she now had in her life once was something that she hoped and dreamed of. This was also why she kept the fire of dreams alive in her heart despite having achieved so much. She suffered from the dreamer's disease, which never let her give up on her infinite pursuits. Melinda's situation was similar to Isabella's. The both of them witnessed a tough childhood, but the optimism in their hearts fueled their fulfillment. The issues they faced were adverse, but their will to get back stronger was greater.

Even though she was drained from the coaching weekend, Isabella found herself comforted as the ladies hopped on to the call. After the break, Isabella and Melinda desperately looked forward to their listening call scheduled for Tuesday.

Isabella expressed herself, saying, "Do you ever wonder, Melinda, if it weren't for our incredible dreams, life would be so ordinary? Personally, I think it is the possibility of turning my hopes into reality that makes me go on. The experience I have had in life dictates that there are endless possibilities for achievements. I don't think there is anything I would set my heart on, and it cannot be true. Only a matter of time, and my dedication makes it likely or unlikely."

Melinda replied, portraying her enthusiasm for what Isabella uttered, "I completely agree. If anything, life has shown me the same. This reminds me of the book I once read. It mentioned a quote that said something like, 'The possibility of having a dream come true makes life interesting.' When I came to ponder over it, I found the quotes' connection to the life I've spent. If I hadn't dreamt of being in the state I am in right now, all this would be a mere illusion. It would stay in my head without ever being real."

Isabella has always yearned for a balance between her spirituality and practicality. She believed in science to get closer to religion; unlike other people, she could see a profound connection between them. Isabella knew that this balance would add meaning to her life; she didn't wish for anything too much or too little, but just enough. Her desire for balance opened her mind to several notions, such as quantum entanglement and infinite realities. Upon closer examination, it is clear that the concept of 'infinite worlds' does not only exist in many cultures, but it is also backed up by science to an extent.

Many tales and legends originated in our world, but the truth behind them will forever remain unknown to us. Perhaps this is because we all have different capacities for believing. To say that, to each their own, seems reasonable. The Mandela Effect emerged from Sofia Broome, a paranormal researcher who thought Nelson Mandela had died in prison in the 1980s.

However, the reality was contrary to this claim because Mandela's death didn't occur until 2013. Broome witnessed that it wasn't only her who remembered Mandela's death; many others reported remembering it. What is shocking is the fact that so many people believed watching news coverage reporting his death and similar details of the incident. Since then, the Mandela effect has been known to have some association with the idea that we are already living in an alternate reality with different realities shaped according to our perception.

In light of this tale, the 'Many Worlds Theory' has been a controversial yet interesting area of discussion in the science community. One can't blame the scientists for this because the intricate complexities of the phenomenon make it challenging to derive a conclusion. However, for a layman, the theory behind it sounds pretty intriguing, and it might have much to do with our dreams. Most of us are familiar with Erwin Schrodinger's famous cat experiment. Let's dive into it to understand how its knowledge can shape and impact our thoughts and lives. Schrodinger provides a hypothesis when he places a cat in a box and turns on the nozzle of a poisonous gas. For an ordinary person, it seems straightforward that the cat would die when the box is opened. However, some people like Schrodinger have an ever-lasting quench for knowledge, so naturally, they can't be satisfied with what appears on the surface. Schrodinger proposed that until the box lid is opened, the cat is dead and alive. This led him to develop the idea that upon opening the lid, he would either experience 'sadness' or 'happiness.' Without further complicating it, the suggestion that Erwin Schrodinger makes is the possibilities that exist and are unknown without actually experiencing them. So, until the lid opens, there is no way to determine whether the cat is 'alive' or 'dead' and whether it would make Schrodinger 'happy' or 'sad.' This principle led to the idea of infinite possibilities occurring in infinite universes. The notion is that many unseen universes exist with different outcomes, hence the 'Many Worlds Theory.'

The derivative here would be that every choice we consciously make or every thought we have in this world somehow impacts another universe where the outcomes are different. By that logic, every goal we set in our mind yields a positive result in one of the universe. Why not make it happen in the one you are practically living in? And if you reflect on this for a bit, believing in this theorem means you have absolutely nothing to lose and everything to gain. People who live for the latter part are the ones who make the cut in the race for success.

The relationship between science and spirituality is not alien to those who think with an open mind. During this week's call, Isabella and Melinda spiraled into discussions like these, not realizing how and where the time went by. The call concluded on a disturbing note when Isabella inquired about Cassie's rescue horses. After the call, the ladies decided that they would resume their session this coming Thursday.

"Melinda, you mentioned the rescue horses Cassie looked forward to welcoming. Have they arrived yet?" Isabella asked curiously.

Melinda replied, "I have still been waiting and waiting. This is quite unusual; it's never happened before. I'm sure they would have a good excuse for it because Cassie is losing it over this. Let's hope for the best. What else can we do, right?"

The call ended, and the women returned to their usual chores and business. Isabella felt a wave of passion taking over her body. After the day's work, she spent the evening reminiscing about the call she had with Melinda. She thought of what they were discussing earlier. "With every conversation with Melinda, I can feel an unusual connection I have never experienced before. I have always been a huge believer in quantum entanglement. I guess Melinda's arrival in my life is a testament to that belief."

Quantum entanglement is the idea that when two particles become entangled, they instantly affect each other's properties regardless of their physical distance. What is fascinating is the fact that these connections between particles occur at random. Applying the same principle to our existence, we are connected through an invisible knot with each other. The New York Times explains the original study named Twins Reared Apart: A Living Lab.[3] The study portrays two identical twins, James Arthur Springer and James Edward Lewis, who were separated at birth and reunited thirty-nine years later. The twins showed unbelievable similarities even after being unaware of each other's existence for a span of almost four decades. Their first wives were named Linda, and the second was named Betty. Additionally, these men had grown up with their adopted brothers, who were called Larry. Not only this, but there were many more parallels that would compel anyone to the fact that quantum entanglement occurs not only in particles but also in humans.

Isabella slept on these thoughts, thinking about the fascinating implications of the twin study. Little did she know that the week had shocking revelations for her. There was an unexpected turn of events that would further strengthen her bond with Melinda. At this point, it's hard to say whether it'd be for the good or bad, but knowing the nature of these two women, they could battle any storm they are presented with.

Isabella woke up fresh on a Wednesday morning. She thought about the previous day's happening and felt a surge of tranquility take over her mind. She was well-rested and felt relieved even though she knew that her day would be tiring. Moreover, Isabella couldn't help but notice her ability to be grounded and attentive. Of course, she was no stranger to the reason why. Every time she had a call with Melinda, this feeling was bound to occur. Anyhow, she went on to address her responsibilities for the day. She was busy throughout the day, but there was something that kept her mind occupied. Isabella couldn't seem to find the link, but she had unusual instincts that seemed to worry her.

We are pretty familiar with Isabella's intuitive prowess. Her feelings about something not being right were, in fact, true. As soon as she got up to indulge herself in Thursday's activities, the receptionist at her equestrian facility

---

[3] https://www.nytimes.com/1979/12/09/archives/twins-reared-apart-a-living-lab.html

notified Isabella of a suspicious call she had received from a horse trailer driver. According to the driver, they had been stranded in a downtown city area while transporting horses from the South. The receptionist at the equestrian facility and Isabella both doubted the driver's statement. The driver had told them they needed a suitable route to bring the horse trailers, even though it was a typical city with narrow streets and buildings everywhere. Isabella was stunned for a split second, but she knew she had to think of something immediately. At the moment, she was both confused and agitated by what the driver had said. Isabella had her mind all over the place.

This call would take Isabella on a rollercoaster of events. This call had to do something with Melinda, not only Isabella. These women were persistent in their beliefs regarding quantum entanglement, but little did they know that they were about to encounter this theoretical idea in their practical lives. This call would lead to a series of unanticipated circumstances that Isabella or Melinda could never imagine, even in their dreams. However, one thing is definite – everything that Isabella and Melinda believed in, individualistically or collaboratively, was about to unfold in front of their eyes. We don't know the certainty of future events, but we do know one thing –  Isabella and Melinda would now be more inclined than ever to work with their spirit animals. Their belief in the bond they shared would be consolidated beyond words, uniting them through unexpected horizons.

# V

# The Stranded Horses

We, humans, understand love only in the capacities of our perception. The concept of love is not new to us. It has been part of the early human history and prevails across global cultures. However, our beliefs and definitions of love vary, to a point where it's safe to agree that love is a subjective area of discussion. On the other hand, it's also a subject that ignites a wave of enthusiasm in us and makes us better in some ways. For us, love can be perceived as a feeling of care, affection, and understanding between people.

Love can exist beyond the notions of time, space, and matter.

This brings us to assume the love Isabella had for horses. More than love, it was her prowess to feel their pain as strongly as if it were hers. The calls her facility had received about the horses left her in deep distress. Isabella searched her contacts and found an old friend in animal control. Serrah previously used to board Isabella's horses. Isabella sounded severely upset when she called Serrah regarding the horses. Serrah was more than eager to help her friend out, so she assured Isabella and told her that she would soon be on her way to investigate the situation herself. The sketchiness of the situation was already no alien to Isabella, but Serrah's instincts could also not deny it. Now, Serrah was on her route and although her call comforted Isabella to an extent, her empathy and care for the horses was rather involuntary.

Isabella called the drivers and let them know that Serrah was coming to get the horses off the trailer and safely to the equestrian facility. As soon as Serrah arrived at the horses, Isabella's suspicions were proved right. The horses were brutally stranded there for days without nourishment. What worried Serrah and Isabella more was that their condition indicated something more serious. The poor animals looked entirely dehydrated and starved. In light of the situation, Serrah and Isabella mutually decided that it was pragmatic for them to bring the horses to Isabella's farm where the horses would properly be monitored. Serrah put down the phone after letting Isabella know that it would take her thirty minutes to reach the farm.

Human perception of time can be seriously complicated. The most precious and the happiest moments in life pass by in a jiff. But the time when we are put under emotional pressure or a daunting circumstance, our patience gives in. The smallest unit of time is the zeptosecond, which is the trillionth of a billionth of a second. You might be wondering who would really ponder that much about this, but Isabella sure was. She kept overthinking and spiraling. She could not find herself patient in light of the current situation. All she wished was for the horses to arrive at the farm so she could help them get better. It's as if she could exactly feel the brutality that they had been put under.

It was late evening, and the barn staff had left the farm. Isabella made do with the resources that were accessible to her and took help from the employees from the front office. They prepared each stall with fresh bedding, ample hay, and five buckets of water. Although they had automatic waterers for horses, some would prefer the manual system and with the conditions these horses were under, Isabella wouldn't dare leave the slightest chance for their discomfort.

Isabella was reminiscing about her entire journey and everything she learned from her experience with horses. She could not help her emotions thinking how much a horse's presence makes one feel calm and serene.

She was lost deep in her thoughts, "The world may be filled with chaos and confusion, but nothing can go wrong when you're surrounded by horses. They are filled with the tranquility and understanding that we spend our lives searching for. How can one be this cruel to these harmless creatures? How do people look at themselves in a mirror after they torture an innocent creature who doesn't react to the torture? Are they made without a conscience? Hate is a strong word, but I'm so angry..."

Isabella was so occupied with the day's happening that she almost forgot about the listening call that was due today. Her spiraling thoughts were interrupted by Melinda's call. After greeting her, Melinda asked Isabella how she was doing. This rarely occurred, if ever. Isabella and Melinda both strictly abided by the call's professional nature and didn't wind up on random conversations. The two of them were dedicated to the assignment and were sure not to direct the call elsewhere. However, today, Isabella couldn't contain her agitation. As soon as she heard Melinda asking about her well-being, Isabella felt compelled to fill her in with the emotionally charging events of the day.

"Melinda, there are eight horses stranded in a trailer that is fit to support only four. Imagine the agony that these poor animals are facing right now. I don't mean to dump this all on you but the frustration I have been feeling all day and even as we speak is beyond words. That's what I was busy thinking about before you called; how can any human be so merciless to the innocent beings? Are they not scared of the wrath of God?"

Melinda listened very carefully; if anything, she empathized with Isabella. She was patient and sensitive to Isabella's situation, but she gradually revealed something even more concerning.

She told Isabella, "I don't mean to draw any conclusions here, but something seems to be common here, Isabella. Cassie received a call from one of the trailer drivers and they revealed something about her horses being stuck in New Jersey when they were being brought to her farm in Massachusetts. Let's hope everything is well."

Isabella pondered over the situation and said, "Ugh. This is rather disturbing, Melinda. Can one of the horses be yours? But that's not possible. I think I'm not in the right headspace to decide anything right now. Can we please reschedule this call for another day? In the meantime, send me a picture of your horse, okay? I'll confirm and update you with whatever I find out at my earliest. For now, we can only hope and pray that the poor babies are brought to my farm safely. I wouldn't let a fly near them the minute they step foot in my shelter. I have their stalls prepped with ample food and water. I want them to arrive here as soon as possible.

Melinda agreed with Isabella and said, "Yes, I'm hoping for the best as well, Isabella. You don't worry so much and look out for yourself, okay? Everything is going to fall into place. We can surely reschedule this call for another time. Get the horses all the necessary care and affection, from my side too. You can't take their pain, but you're trying your best and that's all that matters."

The ladies dropped the call; what Melinda said was worrying Isabella. She wanted to make sure if one of the horses was the one Cassie ordered. The trailer arrived in the meantime. As they started unloading the horses, Isabella was struck by the terrible conditions these horses were under. Isabella could evidently notice from the faces of these horses how desperate they were to get out of there. She looked into their eyes with patience as if she was trying to comfort them. Isabella, with her empathetic understanding, didn't need words to build a relationship with the horses. As each of the horses was unloaded from the trailer, Isabella looked into their eyes and told them, "Hey, buddy; you're safe now. Nobody can hurt you here." Her eyes got a little watery and she was overwhelmed seeing her spirit animals in that condition. As enraged and aggravated as Isabella was in the moment because of what had happened, she didn't express her anger in front of the trailer drivers. She knew she had to keep her calm and not trigger them because she didn't want to cause a scene there. Moreover, she was also worried that they'd take the horses away if she said anything to them. All Isabella could think of was how grateful she was that the animals were now safely under her surveillance. The animal control officers accompanied Isabella until the drivers were off to their hotels for the rest of the evening. They waved Isabella a fine goodbye and told her that they would pick up the horses in the morning.

"The hell you would!" Isabella faked a smile with all she had left, but inside she was burning with rage. There wasn't a chance that she would give the horses away to the drivers after seeing how poorly they were treated.

As worked up as she had been, the night's tranquility contrasted with the day's chaotic nature. She was weighed down by extreme exhaustion, but the melodic sound of the horses drinking and eating provided her ease. Her heart throbbed with painful empathy as she wondered at the horse's condition, but a wave of hope stirred within her as she saw these animals stand resilient in the face of human cruelty. The faculty, although a few were available, made it possible along with Isabella to ensure that the horses were taken care of in the best possible parameters after they arrived at the farm.

Isabella kept looking at the horses with a faint smile. She stood there for as long as her thoughts dictated her, "These resilient animals teach us so much about fighting adversity. Even though they were put under the worst, these heavenly creations possess so much strength. Their eyes reflect love after so much that happened to them. They looked at me as if they found hope through my eyes. I know love exists because these horses fill my heart with so much of it."

Isabella's thoughts were interrupted when she recalled Melinda's words on the call earlier. She wondered if one of the horses could be the same one that Cassie ordered to rescue. Isabella could brush this question inside the label of a coincidence, but her mind was beyond such assumptions. Everything in her life was interconnected and she was persistent that Melinda's friendship served a purpose that would unfold only with time.

How would the horse's arrival impact Isabella and Melinda's friendship? Perhaps this was a collective manifestation of their calling; something that was central to Isabella and Melinda's bond. We don't know yet, but knowing Isabella and Melinda, they would do whatever it takes to make the best out of the situation, no matter how tragic.

# VI

# A Promise to Protect

We, humans, protect those we love. Protection is a form of love that comes naturally. We spoke of having different perceptions about love; protection is one of them. Some people tend to express love through control, while others simply want to provide everything their loved ones might need and more. Knowing the difference between the former and the latter is essential. When we exert control over someone we love, it signifies that we fear losing them. It makes our love selfish. However, love is when you disregard your personal needs and offer everything it takes for them to be happy.

Isabella's love was reserved for her horses. She loved them unconditionally, and more than she loved them, she wanted to keep them safe. Her heart cried over what she had witnessed the night before.

*With a mission to get these horses to their destination, she offered them a promise to protect.*

Isabella's love for the horses is reflected in her concern for them. Although the horses had been rescued the night before, Isabella could not afford to lose them to the horrible trailer drivers once again. She could sense it in the horses' eyes how much they felt at peace with her. She knew the empathy she had for these innocent souls was not shared by others. Isabella became frustrated and agitated in the morning as she thought about last night's events. Nothing was as important to her as protecting the horses that were in her barn.

She woke up early in the morning to ensure they had been properly fed. She looked at them quietly and noticed the serenity on their faces. Isabella wondered how anyone could treat these animals so mercilessly. Isabella was lost in her thoughts when she realized she needed to make sure the horses were fed.

Isabella thought to herself, "I have to take care of them myself. These poor beings have gone through so much in the past few days. I must make sure that I attend to all their needs. They deserve all the love present in the world and more."

She got the buckets of water and fed them, telling them, "You are safe here with me. No one can hurt you, and I'll make sure of that. I am going to protect you forever from all the evil in this world."

Isabella's empathy for the horses cannot be expressed enough. Someone else would call it madness, but Isabella knew that horses could listen, perhaps even better than us. She looked into their eyes with utmost compassion and sincerity. Her heart cried for their suffering. She made sure that each horse present in her stalls knew that they were sheltered and cared for at her facility. Isabella had ensured that everything was in place for the horses to feel safe. She took care of their nutritional and emotional needs. She visited them in the barn occasionally, constantly making sure that they were fine.

Isabella was hanging around in the barn when she got a call from the trailer drivers that they were coming to pick up the horses. Isabella's tone got apparently stern as she heard them say that. She said, "Let me get back to you on this, alright? My facility is taking care of the horses for now. I'll contact you if we need you to do anything more than you already have."

One could notice the anger behind the last remark. Isabella, having a calm nature, did not like to cause unnecessary chaos. However, this situation was already chaotic. She didn't want the trailer drivers to drop by. She would never let that happen, at least not under her watch. Isabella contacted the local and county authorities. She explained last night's scenario to them and asked them if she could keep them in her facility. She assured them that she was already set on a mission to find their owners and would get them back to them. The county representatives understood her; they were sorry for what happened with the horses. Isabella felt comfortable after knowing that the trailer drivers could not take the horses away from her.

Knowing that the horses were safe in her custody, Isabella visited them for the last time before leaving. She looked at each of the horses and told them, "I don't know how you ended up on my doorstep, but my promise to you is that your suffering comes to an end here and now." She found herself a bit teary as she left the horses. However, Isabella couldn't help but wonder about her shared connection with them.

A wave of gratitude took over her as she realized that this might be God's plan. She was a huge believer that things don't occur at random. She believed in the concept of interconnectedness. Now, her faith has become stronger than ever. As she reminisced about every event in her life, she could not help but rejoice at the fact that she was getting closer to her purpose with every passing day.

When we speak of our calling, we tend to think of superficial things. We assume that our calling exists in exploring the mysteries of the universe or hidden parts of the galaxy; something nobody has done before. We set our expectations so high that when we don't reach them, we find ourselves weeping in disappointment.

What if we change the direction in which we seek our purpose?

It can be as little as protecting someone—something similar to what Isabella did for her horses. We often forget that our purpose might be hidden in some place that looks ordinary but is, in fact, special.

Finding a purpose in this life seems an impossible task for many. *Ever wondered why?*

Is it because it isn't strong enough to be pursued? Or is it that we aren't aligned with our best selves? Well, there is no definitive answer here, but we can say that our purpose requires us to keep our minds open to change. It is the evolution that granted humans the state they are in at present. It is infused in the very nature of humans, so why refute it? Of course, changes are not comfortable, at least not at first. However, our ability to adapt to different circumstances helps us grow. Maybe this is our purpose in life—to experience and adapt every moment to its maximum capacity.

Knowing about Isabella's life, we know how versatile she is. The way she handled the difficult situation with the stranded horses is truly admirable. Obviously, she did not particularly fancy the adverse circumstances, but she went through it with courage. She made everything suitable for the animals she loved so much. Isabella could not help but think about it.

She thought to herself, "It is true that God works in mysterious ways. Maybe this was something I was chosen for—to protect the horses. It was indeed sad to see the poor souls go through so much, but now that I think about it, I wonder about their resilient spirits. They continued to keep the kindred spirits alive after being tortured brutally. Being around horses provides me with the resilience I could otherwise not have. It's as if they can read our minds. In order to do so, one has to be in tune with themselves. I have seen it rarely, if ever, when a human has made me feel this way. This surge of tranquility that horses provide me with goes beyond words. How can I ever back out from protecting them? They have given me so much. They added a purpose to my life and aligned me with the manifestations of my soul."

Just as Isabella was gathering her thoughts, she saw her phone ringing. It was Melinda. Isabella had forgotten entirely about their listening session amid the chaos. She was relieved to see Melinda's name on her phone. She could not wait to speak to her.

Isabella answered the call and said, "Hey, Melinda. I'm so glad you called. I had completely brushed your call off my mind between the chaotic events of yesterday."

Melinda answered, "Oh no, honey. You don't have to be sorry about anything. I understand; I could sense in your tone how worried you were last night. You didn't sound yourself. I'd never seen you like this before, but considering how terrible the situation was, if I were you, I would've been in the same state. But how are you? Did you get to rest well?"

Isabella replied, "Yeah, I did. Do you know one of the trailer drivers had the audacity to call me to ask if he could pick up the horses? It aggravated me, honestly. Anyway, enough of this discussion; I don't want to ruin my mood over it anymore. Let me tell you something less disturbing, Melinda. You should've seen the horses who landed in my barn yesterday. Before going to bed, I was looking at them. I lost track of time, but Melinda, do you ever feel that horses can talk to us? I certainly felt it last night and this morning, too. I mean, I was feeding them while telling them that they were safe with me. I could feel them hearing me out, perhaps even better than any person has. The way they looked at me made me feel whole. I was thinking about this before you called. The brutality they faced in the past few days, if it was us in their place, we would've lost our calm. I know I would. They still had so much tranquility on their face. I know it seemed as if I was the one protecting them, but I feel like it was them who protected me from the overwhelming emotions. I could not have been positive if it weren't for them."

Melinda exhaled a blissful sigh, touched by the endearing moment, "I know exactly how you feel, Isabella. Being around horses makes me wonder about the same. I feel blessed to be able to breathe the same air as them. And at this point, I am pretty sure that this is why the universe made us cross each other's paths. Our shared love for horses, similar beliefs, nuanced perceptions, intuitive thoughts, and a drive to constantly evolve—these are the signs. You and I were always meant to be friends. Our majestic little beauties made it happen, and I couldn't be more glad about it."

Isabella smiled as she heard Melinda utter those words.

After exchanging some warm sentiments, Melinda asked Isabella, "Isabella, the last time we spoke, you said you were going to compare my horse's picture with the ones you rescued. I'm guessing the rescue horses don't include mine?"

Isabella replied immediately, "Oh, Melinda, dear! I'm really sorry about that; I have been so occupied with my thoughts that I completely forgot about it. Let me get home, and I'll do that instantly. Now that I have spoken to you, I feel relatively at ease. What do you say?"

Melinda, "No worries at all. Fill me in with the update. I hope to see you soon."

The call ended, and Isabella continued with her day's activities. There was a disturbing thought lingering at the back of her head—she knew it would vanish when she compared the rescue horses with Melinda's picture.

# VII

# A Shocking Discovery

Isabella was headed to the equestrian facility. During her drive, she couldn't help but reflect on the role horses played in her life. Isabella was one for staying true to herself, but she wondered if that would be possible for her if she didn't explore equine therapy. Her thoughts unfolded with one thing leading to another. This took her mind off the troublesome call she had with Melinda about the rescue horses. Soon, Isabella found herself entangled in her thoughts. This allowed her to relax for a while and took her mind off the horses in her barn waiting to be reunited with their owners.

We live in a world where advocating the truth is experienced way more than practicing it. We encounter many people who talk about admiring the truth. Some may even express their immense hatred for lies. However, if you contemplate, do we always speak the truth? Forget about others and think about the lies you've told during the last week.

"I had to skip school because my grandma is sick"

"I am late because of the heavy traffic."

These might sound familiar. These are the lies all of us have uttered. It's nothing to be embarrassed about because, at one point in our lives, we have lied to stay out of trouble. Everyone does, and this isn't what we are saying; psychology confirms it. The neuroscience behind lying behavior has been explored by many researchers. Cross River Therapy conducted research to observe lying patterns in their respondents and, consequently, found out that people, in fact, lie a lot. Seventy-five percent of their respondents told zero to two lies per day.[4] This figure might not sound like a big deal at its face value, but that's a lot of lies.

Zety's 2020 research interviewed a thousand participants and concluded that ninety-six percent of them lied to escape work responsibilities.[5]

But why do people feel the need to lie? Is it to stay out of trouble or simply because of the lack of morals? Well, one can say it's a combination of several distinct factors. Most times, we lie to stay out of trouble or protect ourselves and the ones we hold dear. We also lie to maintain a reputation for ourselves.

However, the most dangerous lies we tell are to ourselves. This lying pattern is not always conscious; it might be hidden in the deepest parts of our unconscious brain. Without knowing, you might be hiding the truth from yourself. This is perhaps because we're often terrified of looking in the mirror. The truth is often brutal for us to face, so we find comfort in concealing it. We keep falling into an endless loop of deceiving ourselves, but truth has a way of catching up. No matter how good you are at hiding the truth, one day, it will show you an honest reflection.

---

[4] https://www.crossrivertherapy.com/research/lying-statistics#:~:text=On%20a%20daily%20occurrence%2C%20there,when%20talking%20to%20their%20physicians.

[5] https://www.forbes.com/sites/christinecomaford/2020/10/17/why-we-lie-and-the-neuroscience-behind-it/#:~:text=Bella%20DePaulo%2C%20Ph.,lasting%2010%20or%20more%20minutes.

Fyodor Dostoevsky once said, *"Your worst sin is that you have been destroyed and betrayed yourself for nothing."*

The depth of this quote subtly hits the hearts of those who have spent a lifetime practicing it. Deceiving yourself is far worse than deceiving others. You don't necessarily lie to yourself for its sake. Often, lying to yourself means putting others' needs above yours. Or making everyone else happy while compromising your boundaries. This is where self-reflection comes into play. It aligns you with your best interests. Not only is reflecting on your inner self essential for you, but also has to do something with the role you play in others' lives. Someone who is fully aware of their needs and wants is likely to make the people around them happy. You're likely to be content with who you are, and it makes you resilient.

In this regard, equine therapy holds the mirror of truth for you to reflect on yourself. It adds depth to your perception and helps you practice compassion with yourself.

Spending massive time around horses and nurturing them made Isabella and Melinda know themselves in the best possible way. These women are distinguished in many areas of life and this was a gift that their treasured animals gave them.

A blog by Equine Lead LLC summarizes the various ways in which horses help us recognize our truth.[6] These innocent creatures might not know how to communicate with us in the language we speak, but they are intuitively aligned with our thoughts. For example, during equine therapy, a person encounters an emotionally turbulent conversation on a phone call. Upon cutting the call, they engage with the horse, pretending to seem okay, but the horse walks away. The horse is trying to signal an important message to the

---

[6] http://www.equinelead.com/blog/how-can-horses-help-you-learn-about-yourself

person. They reject the negativity and try to disassociate from their surroundings. The horse can very well read the person's body language to know that they are upset. Through their behavior, the horse lets the person know to catch up with it once they've cleansed their aura of the negative interaction. Once the person realizes why the horse might be getting away from them, they take a brief moment to reflect on their energy, take a few deep breaths, and try to engage with the horse again. In turn, the horse begins to feel at ease and lets the person in their space.

Although they don't speak our language, horses reveal a lot about reading the surroundings to us. They observe and react to our non-verbal cues to help us understand ourselves in a better way.

This solves the mystery of the profound characters Isabella and Melinda hold today. More importantly, the more we explore the behaviors of horses, the more it tells us why these women considered them their spirit animals.

Upon reaching the equestrian center, Isabella raced to the horses. She looked at the picture of Melinda's horse and compared it to the ones in her barn. At first, she couldn't find any similarities, but she kept looking until she was confident that the horse wasn't Melinda's. It wasn't easy to find any similarities because Melinda's picture represented a healthy horse, while the ones in her barn were not as healthy. However, Isabella saw an inarguable brand on one of the horse's left flanks. This was an amazing discovery, this was the horse in the picture from Melinda. Isabella felt a surge of discomfort as she looked at the condition of the horse that arrived at her door and that turned out to be her friend's horse. Melinda expected the horse to be in the same condition as the picture versus its present poor health. She could not help but feel anger at the ones who brought these poor souls into this condition.

"I can be angry about this sometime later, but right now, I must update Melinda with this news." Isabella thought to herself.

She called Melinda to let her know of this. Isabella felt uncomfortable telling Melinda about the condition of her horse. However, she knew that she ultimately had to let her know. Isabella was also aware that Melinda wouldn't be happy hearing about that he was safe. Melinda answered the call after two rings.

"Hey, Isabella, I was just about to call you. Honestly, I'm getting a little impatient about the horse. I hope there's nothing to worry about." Melinda said.

"Melinda, hey! I completely understand your agitation. I would feel the same if I was in your position. And yeah, I did find out about the horses. One of them belongs to you, but he doesn't look a tad bit similar to the picture you sent me. The poor guy is in fragile health. It looks half the size of how it used to be. I'm really sorry about this, Melinda. I knew this isn't something you wanted to hear." Isabella replied.

Melinda replied with a heaviness in her tone, "You don't have to apologize, Isabella. You did whatever you could. As sad I am to hear about this, I'm thanking God that you found it before someone else. Were you able to locate all of them to their respective owners?"

Isabella replied, sharing Melinda's sadness, "You're the first one. I'm onto finding the others, but seeing their condition, I have to make sure that they are in perfect health before they can be transported elsewhere. I've called medical help to get them checked and then I'll get them back to their owners. Is it okay with you if I keep your horse under my supervision for a few days?"

Melinda answered, "Yeah, I'm more than fine with it. I know how protective you are of these horses. If there's anyone I trust with their care more than myself, it's you. I have complete faith in you, Isabella."

This shocking discovery further strengthened Isabella and Melinda's bond. Although they would never actively want the horses to be hurt, the women shared their despair over this event. The torture these horses were put through was felt deeply by Isabella and Melinda.

After cutting the call, Isabella looked at Melinda's horse. She could feel the pain in his eye. She resented the humans who brought them such agony. Isabella was careful not to transmit her feelings to the horses. She was acutely aware that they would sense the hatred she was facing. However, she also understood that they could understand her empathy for them. By being there for them during this time, Isabella developed an emotional connection with them. She knew they could hear her emotions as strongly as she felt them.

In the previous chapters, we spoke about quantum entanglement in detail. We are clearly aware of Isabella's intrigue and belief in this theory. While she was furious about the treatment these poor animals had received, she knew they didn't arrive at her doorstep out of a coincidence. Isabella was fully informed that things don't occur at random. She knew that the horses in her barn were a result of her manifestation. It was her yearning to keep the horses protected and sheltered that brought them to her doorstep.

Isabella took a deep inhale and let her worries go. Looking at the horses provided her hope. Nothing could comfort Isabella except witnessing the resilient spirits the horses embodied. They were the epitome of courage.

She let out a sigh and calmed herself, "If they can go through the severe pain inflicted upon them and still portray serenity, I can too. I have to stay strong for them if not for myself. I must not let my emotions get in the way of their well-being. I'll find a way to contain this intense hatred I feel. I have an essential task to accomplish; I must ensure to get these horses back to their homes. That's the only thing that matters to me right now; everything else can wait."

# VIII

# Unmasking the Truth

The drivers arrived with the trailers to take the horses back. Isabella looked at the deplorable condition of the horses. She remained baffled by their audacity to come for the horses after they treated them brutally for days.

"How can I ever find it in myself to let them go with these drivers?" She thought. She didn't want to express her emotions in front of the drivers because doing so would compromise the horse's well-being. And nothing else at the moment meant more to Isabella than keeping her companions safe. She did not trust anyone else besides herself for their protection. Especially after the way the horses arrived at Isabella's barn, completely dehydrated and without food, Isabella was determined to keep them safe, and would not let her guard down.

Isabella felt stress taking over her. She imagined the route they took from the highway to Canada, nearly two thousand miles filled with terror and uncertainty, not to mention unbearable hunger and thirst.. She was terrified to the core. She felt a rush of disbelief in humans who let innocent animals be victims of senseless torture. Isabella was angry, sad, and horrified at the same time. She let out a deep sigh and tried not to reveal the emotions she was experiencing at the moment.

Struggling to hide her feelings, Isabella looks in the eyes of the horses. A burst of serenity takes over her mind and her determination to protect them becomes stronger.

Isabella made calls to the local authorities in an attempt to get rid of the trailer drivers. Despite the agitation she felt toward them, she hides it behind a stern expression. The local authorities advised her of the animal cruelty regulations and to have a veterinarian examine them and determine their health. When the drivers were informed that a veterinarian was coming along with local authorities, they fled the area in a hurry.

She received a call from Melinda, saying, "Hey, Isabella, I hope you're doing well. I just called to check up on you and to tell you that when I told Casey about the horses being under your supervision, she was thrilled. I can't believe but she seems to trust you. She looked very happy and satisfied when I told her. And if I said I didn't love the idea, I'd be lying too. I've seen the way you are super protective of the horses around you. You treat them as if they're your children."

Isabella replied, "Hey, Melinda, I'm delighted to hear that honestly. Give Casey my warm regards and tell her that as long as I'm present, I wouldn't let anything bad happen to the horses. However, I feel compelled to tell you about the trailer driver who just left. They were here to pick the horses; can you believe the guts they have? After keeping them without food and water for days, they expected me to allow them to leave with the horses. You have no idea about the amount of energy it took for me to hide my emotions. Deep inside, I was burning with rage."

Melinda empathized with Isabella and told her, "You are a smart woman, Isabella. You did right by keeping your feelings to yourself. And the way they treated the horses, they had no right to come back for them. I am baffled at the cruelty of this world."

"The greatness of a nation and its moral progress can be judged by the way its animals are treated."

This quote belongs to a legendary man who taught us many things about the fight for justice. When you reflect on it, the truth behind this quote seems real. The selfishness of human nature enables us to inflict torture upon innocent creatures who can't speak for themselves. Horses have proved themselves to be great human companions for as long as we can remember. They have supported us during war times, in hunting, and for transport. They have stayed our allies for over five thousand years, remaining an ever-present companion during war and peace. Before the technical advancements in steam locomotive, horses were there for us, providing us the means to travel from one place to the other. Additionally, contemporary times are no alien to horses' companionship and assistance. They have been a part of equine therapy, something that teaches us to reach our higher selves.

But have we, as humans, done justice to the unwavering support these animals provided us? Most certainly not. Let alone gratitude; the way we treat them after all their support is a testament to our self-absorbed nature.

Isabella's morality rejects the idea that she should let the horses get away with the drivers. She had made a promise to protect them, and she would keep it until her very last breath. She wouldn't leave them alone on their journey.

Isabella is well-aware of the transformative journey that the horses put her through. She strongly believed that connection with them was beyond words; it worked on an intuitive level. She decided to spend time with her guardian animals before she went searching for their owners. Multiple thoughts crossed her mind while looking at them.

The seventeenth century is generally regarded as the Age of Enlightenment. It was a period where we saw science, logic, and reasoning take over religious and spiritual ideologies. However, can we really regard it as a period of enlightenment while leaving our core behind? A 1918 sociologist, Max Weeber, perceptively said that we had entered an era of mirages and illusions, a world that doesn't hold any meaning beyond the obvious. In this light, he said, *"As intellectualism suppresses belief in magic, the world's processes become disenchanted, lose the magical significance, and henceforth simply 'are' and 'happen' but no longer signify anything."*

The Age of Enlightenment slowly led us towards 'reductionist materialism,' a perception that believes science contains the answers to everything present in the universe. Mulling over it, don't you think this theory takes the magic out of our lives?

In this regard, Blaise Pascal's view about God counterargues with the notion of reductionist materialism. According to Pascal, believing in God leaves us with nothing to lose and everything to gain. He said, "If God does not exist, one loses nothing by believing in him anyway, while if he does exist, one stands to lose everything by not believing."

While empirical science involves itself in data collection, external observation, and evaluation, quantum physics connects the divide between science and spirituality. Quantum entanglement or what Einstein regarded as "Spooky action at distance," embodies the idea of interconnectedness more than any other principle. It suggests that two particles, when entangled, can be far away from each other in the universe and still remain connected. This theory demonstrates to us that information travels across the boundaries of space and time.

We don't know about rest, but we do know that Isabella does not only believe in this mere theory; she lives and breathes it. Reminiscing about the happenings of the past few days, she realizes how much horses have taught her about interconnectedness. She recalls the horses' arrival on her doorstep, Melinda's horse being among them, and her duty to protect them. Isabella feels that she had related to these horses even before they had met. She rejoices at the bond that exists between them and is proud of herself for being their voice.

Isabella looks into one of the horse's eyes and tells them, "You and I are each other's companion, in this life, and in the one we can't see. It's my oath to keep you safe from evil and I will take this oath to my grave."

Just as she's immersed in her thoughts beyond consciousness, her phone rings. Isabella sees Melinda's name on the screen.

"And they say intuition is pseudo-science. Every time I'm lost thinking about an unseen and unheard connection, Melinda calls." She thought to herself as she proceeded to answer Melinda.

"Hey, Melinda, you know what? I was just reading this paper about quantum physics. I loved every word in it. But what's really interesting is the fact that every time I am in between something that talks about spiritual connections, I hear from you. It would be unfair to label it under a coincidence, right?" Isabella expressed.

Melinda seemed to be thrilled by Isabella's words, "Ha! Isabella, nothing in this world is a coincidence. If anything my life has taught me, it's that everything happens for a reason. You might not know of it before, but when you invest time and energy, you realise the answers were always in front of you. I mean, look at the both of us; despite being so aligned with our intuition, could we possibly fathom that one day, you will be tasked to rescue and protect my horse? I sure didn't."

Isabella replied, "You're absolutely right. We label things as coincidence because of our laziness. We don't fancy digging deep into complex ideas, so we make it convenient for ourselves by calling it a happy accident."

The two women chatted for hours and hours without getting tired. Isabella realised how much she needed a few moments of laughter and banter with Melinda. The conversation they had reinvigorated her. After the horrible feelings she had witnessed in the past few days regarding the horses' arrival, Isabella felt grateful for the little moments of peace.

She looked at the horses and felt a shift in her spirit – a transformation shaped by love, empathy, and kindness. She found herself feeling glorified about the incredible road she had traveled. She decided that she had been chosen as a guardian of the gentle souls who had given her so much. Isabella knew that her journey was far from over. She had to reunite the horses with their owners, but more than that, she found herself connecting with the horses on a different level. With every pulse, she sensed the universe echoing her manifestation – to protect, nurture, and advocate the sacred bond between humans and horses. Her pursuit of the mission amplified, and as difficult as the journey might have been until now, Isabella wasn't ready to give up. She would not stop until she unmasked the truth about the horses staying in her barn.

# IX

# Reuniting The Horse And The Owner

As humans, we condition our magical encounters to be wrapped in visibly mystical structures. This is perhaps because we see it according to our perception of beauty. For example, when you hear the term 'magic,' what do you visualize?

Is it a white fairy embodying the essence of an angel?

Or is it a garden filled with sparkling flowers and magical rivers?

Well, this might not be your vision exactly, but somehow, our perception of magic is always cliché.

But take a look around and reflect on your life's journey. We bet that someone who has an eye for perceiving true magic would find themselves surrounded by it. Magic does not necessarily have to be something unbelievable, which is ironic. We aren't talking about the plain act. Instead, we are referring to the magic of life – our treasured connections, the yearnings of the heart that manifest themselves in your reality, and the coincidences – well, a believer would know that nothing in this world is a coincidence. Everything in your life

is a product of your own thoughts. If you ask us, once you experience this magic, you will forget about the beauty that lies on the surface.

Horse Connections through Quantum Entanglement

For Isabella, the definition of magic wasn't restricted to an optical illusion, something that doesn't exist beyond a fictional lens. She considered her entire life to be a beautiful and magical journey. Her wisdom shaped the magic of her life. The encounters she had molded the essence of magic. And the people she met along the way made this magic worth living.

Isabella stood on the edge of the golden bridge as the dusk's embrace wrapped her into its warmth. It creaked subtly under her body weight, a reminder of the numerous storms it had weathered. It extended across a beautiful river reflecting the clear blue sky, its waters flowing, mirroring an image of a horse. As Isabella stood above the beautiful river and under nature's prettiest blanket, she could feel a burden lifting off her chest. She smiled to herself as she mirrored her treasured beings. The horses were more than just animals near her; they were her companions in this life and her teachers for the next one. She paused for a brief second to hear the melodic whispers of the wind, a constant chant that keeps her calm in a chaotic world.

She was surrounded by dimensions that led to her past and present. On one hand, it captured the years of trauma she faced during childhood, and on the other hand, stood her horses, reminding her of resilience at each step. Isabella wanted to hold on to this moment forever. If it was up to her, she would put it in a box and store it for as long as she could.

Isabella's dream was interrupted by the ringing alarm bell. As much as Isabella wanted to put it off, she couldn't. She had to complete her mission of locating the horses to their owners. However, before jumping to the day's tasks, Isabella took a moment to analyze her dream. She had a habit of recalling her dreams right after she woke up.

Dreams capture the reality that we often try to mask from ourselves. They are the mirrors that one cannot crash. Scientifically speaking, dreams are the work of the subliminal parts of our brains, the ones that are not seen. To be more precise, dreams help you know about yourself more than anything else. On the other hand, dreams are often perceived in a spiritual light. By this, we don't mean to refer to the psychics who interpret your future based on your dream. Since they help you get closer to yourself, dreams are closely linked with spirituality, solidifying your relationship with God as you understand him.

*"How we see God is a direct reflection of how we see ourselves; we don't see things as they are, we see them as we are. If God brings to mind mostly fear and blame, it means there is too much fear and blame welled inside us. If we see God as full of love and compassion, so are we."*

Isabella smiled as she opened the book kept on her side table. "Forty rules of love. As much as I read you, it's never enough. You always have something in store for me, something that leaves me with goosebumps." She thought.

Isabella knew that the day ahead of her was going to be hectic. Nevertheless, the dream she had renewed her spirit – she felt as if her magical dream penetrated her with an adrenaline shot, metaphorically speaking, of course. Isabella quickly made her bed and got done with her morning rituals to carry on with the day. She reached her equestrian center to witness her horses silently grazing on the pastures before them.

Isabella quickly hopped on to searching for their respective owners. She used her connections, social media, and a network of local and state officials to unite these horses with their owners. Without realizing it, the day passed in a jiff. Isabella was able to partially achieve her mission. With each hour, Isabella's determination elevated. Out of every day, today, she was infused with a special focus and positive energy that kept her calm throughout the day. She spent the next two days frantically searching for the horses' owners. She made calls upon calls until the work was finished. Luckily, Isabella, along with her facility's unwavering support, was able to locate the man who wanted to sell these horses. As it turns out, this wasn't his first experience with animal cruelty. Previously, the guy had been involved in sketchy activities and was on the wanted list. This news added to Isabella's calmness. She was happy knowing that the horses were now safe and the man responsible for their suffering was held accountable.

Upon finding all the horse owners, Isabella called them and asked them if she could keep the horses under her supervision for a while. Before they were sent home, she wanted to make sure that they were healthy enough to travel. She wanted them to receive a medical clearance check-up to be certain that they were in a condition to travel the long route. By the end of the second day, all the owners were enlightened about the situation. All of them consented to keep the horses in Isabella's facility until they were in perfect health.

Isabella couldn't help but notice the relief in their owners' voices. The feeling of reuniting the horses back with their owners and their homes was inexplicable. The past two days had surely been one heck of a ride, but the results she accomplished made the chase worthwhile. She also felt a surge of sadness at the thought of letting them go.

Isabella thought about the human moral compass that horses brilliantly reflect. She immersed deeply in her thoughts, too zoned out to care about her surroundings.

She thought to herself, "Oh, look how beautiful these creatures look. Every time I see them, they bring me immense happiness. The way they are incapable of lying baffles me. Things must be so simple for them, which is ironic for us because when we lie, we hope to make life simpler when in fact, we are entangling ourselves in our own miseries. We rely on words for understanding and affection, while these beautiful creations of God don't need words at all. We spend our lives searching for ideas like spirituality, but they were created with it; they have it ingrained in them. This reminds me of a quote by Elif Shafak when she says, '*Sufis do not judge other people on how they look or who they are. When a Sufi stares at someone, he keeps both eyes closed, instead opens a third eye — the eye that sees the inner realm.*' How beautiful is this saying? The horses aren't concerned with what appears on the mere surface; instead, they have an unbreakable bond with a person's truth. All they see is through the third eye. It leaves me fascinated thinking about life through their lens. Anyone would be lucky to have that. Moreover, they teach you so much about companionship. If it were a horse's personal decision, they would never live without their herd. Their well-being is dependent on the three Fs: Forage, friends, and freedom. If I think about it, food provides us with serotonin, a happy chemical. Friends are the building blocks of life; they provide us with shelter when the storms are heavy. Without freedom, the essence of a human being is reduced. Everything we humans secretly crave is naturally infused in their system. I don't know on what grounds we think of ourselves as superior beings; it's perhaps because we have the ability to control every other being on this planet, but that's it. We couldn't be near them even if we tried."

Isabella kept looking at the horses in her barn. She reflected on how tiring the past two days had been for her. However, she was humbled by the sight of her spirit creatures. She thought about everything that crossed her mind.

Let's come back to the chapter's opening. You do not need to witness magic in its literal form.

*Transform your thoughts.*

*Open the eye that sees the world with beauty and compassion.*

*Treat others with love.*

*Be the voice of those creatures who don't have a voice.*

*Care for the ones who are incapable of doing so for themselves.*

The magic will flow in your veins. It will fill your heart with boundless love. Just as the sea never goes out of the water, magic will never leave your door.

# X

# Road To Recovery

The fear of losing a loved one and the grief associated with it is often discussed and highlighted on various platforms. But seldom do we talk about the fear of losing a pet—especially four-legged buddies such as horses, loyal companions craving love and attention. What Isabella was going through, witnessing the deteriorating condition of the horses, was inexplicable.

As compassionate and kind as she was, Isabella could not just sit back and watch those beautiful and majestic animals suffer. From the day the horses arrived, she prioritized them. Without a care in the world, she invested her time and attention into tending to their needs. For the horses that were abused and harmed, she became a source of comfort—she was mending something she didn't break!

Each day, she would visit the barn, pat all the horses with tender love, and fulfill their needs. Her treatment of them was proof enough of her compassionate and kind nature. Each horse had its own story of pain; however, under Isabella's supervision, each tale of struggle turned into a story of healing; everyone was comforted.

As a famous quote says, "*Caring for animals is not just an act of kindness; it is a matter of living up to our humanity*," Isabella became a source of comfort for them, making those innocent animals believe in humanity once again.

There was Apollo, who was too thin and terrified when he first arrived, now roamed around the paddock happily, and his eyes were bright with life again. Then, there was Chester, an abandoned baby stallion, now showing signs of joy and mischief by running around playfully around. Then comes Melinda's horse, weak, healing, but no longer looked weaker than when he arrived. Isabella was giving him extra care because he was so fragile when he came that he couldn't even raise his head due to weakness.

Every day, Isabella would come to the barn to fill the feed bins with grain and fresh hay and provide the medication for the horses. She just knew how to pamper and offer tender care to the horses. She knew their love language, like how Apollo would come running to Isabella in the morning for his daily dose of nuzzling, or Chester would perform weird stunts to get Isabella's attention. But since Melinda's horse was weak, he would show his love by resting his face on Isabella's shoulder. Through this, Isabella was not only taking care of the horses but also trying to build their trust in humanity again.

After the mealtime, Isabella would let all the horses play around. Watching them play brought her immense joy. She looks at them and smiles as they run freely in the paddock. It was a sight Isabella had longed to see. It reminded her that even after being stranded in the middle of nowhere and undergoing such a traumatic situation the horses had been through, they had regained their wildness and freedom in their spirit with love and care. For Isabella, every day spent with those horses was a blessing for her. They were her source of pride and happiness!

However, despite Isabella's immense care and love, the horses needed someone to understand the complexity and extent of the effect on their health. Someone who would look deeper into their condition and offer them the medical attention they needed. Isabella consulted Dr. James regarding the horses' health issues. As he entered the barn, he met Isabella, a routine, and continued to check the horses. He checked Chester first, who was more anxious since she had come to the barn. Isabella stood beside Dr. James as he monitored the heart rate, checked his lungs, and palpated her abdomen.

"He is getting better," Dr. James informed Isabella with a smile on his face.

Apollo was next in line; he, too, had gained weight, and his coat was glowing in the soft light filtering through the window. Both Isabella and Dr. James felt happy as they saw the horses recovering from their severe dehydration, malnutrition, and fungal infections when they first arrived at Isabella's doorstep.

Isabella breathed a sigh of relief when she heard that the horses' health was improving. Dr. James then progressed toward Melinda's horse, who showed signs of drowsiness that day. Isabella had called Dr. James primarily because of his deteriorating condition. As the doctor's stethoscope touched his side, Isabella held her breath. She stood back, watching the veterinarian's every move with the intensity of someone whose happiness was about to shatter. There was something in the air—an antiseptic, animal-scented atmosphere where the sunlight was coming through the open door that made everything feel still.

Dr. James checked his mouth, gums, teeth, heartbeat, and lungs methodically to assess his situation.

"He is extremely dehydrated," the vet said, breaking the silence in a firm voice. "It seems that he is still malnourished. I can feel hollow spots towards his spine. He needs to eat!"

The vet further moved to hooves to check signs of infection.

"Fungal infection, too. His immune system is not working properly due to him being malnourished. We need to treat this first," said the vet.

Isabella bit her lip anxiously. Although she had already suspected the infection, hearing this from the doctor in such severe terms was worse than she had imagined.

*Was it too late?*

Will he be able to make it? That's all-what Isabella was thinking about Melinda's horse. Upon asking the vet how long it would take for him to recover, the vet informed him that it would be a week at least until he could be all well. Isabella glanced at the horse again, watching how slowly he could breathe. She felt guilty for the horse to be in such excruciating pain. Isabella swore she'd do whatever it took to get him back on his feet. She couldn't lose him.

As the days passed, Isabella paid attention to Melinda's horse. She kept herself busy comforting her friend's horse. She applied ointments for his fungal infection, gave him medications, and made her eat so that his immunity was boosted. Getting him to eat was getting difficult every day; his ribs were sharp beneath her touch, and his appearance was dull. His health wasn't progressing at all. There were setbacks –- some days, he would not eat or drink anything. She resorted to offering applesauce in hopes that it would spark some kind of interest in food.  On days like that, Isabella couldn't help but feel a sharp tightening in her heart, and the days to come would not be accessible. Ultimately, she decided to administer an IV drip for fluid, changing the bag every two hours.  She kept questioning herself about whether he would be able to make it.

*What if he doesn't? What if, despite everything, I still lose him?*

Questions like these kept her up all night. She could not take her mind off him.

Every morning, Isabella used to go to the barn before sunrise to check all the horses. She used to sit the longest with Melinda's horse. Days when he used to make even the most minor effort, like drinking water, instilled a glimmer of hope in Isabella's heart. It was taking longer, but maybe he will recover. Isabella's consistent care was, indeed, helping. The signs of improvement in his condition were proof enough. His coat was not dull anymore, his body began to appear healthy, and his eyes weren't as hollow as before. Some days, he would eat on his own; Isabella didn't dare to move the bucket because it was after several days that the horse was finally eating. Little progresses like these relieved Isabella; she kept thanking God for it.

As she celebrated his improvements in her heart, she feared that he would stop again. Is this all care even worth it? Is it even curing him?

One day, while spending time in the barn, Isabella whispered in the horse's ear, "We will make it." "Won't we?" The horse nudged at her hand; Isabella smiled with hope in her heart. This was the first day she let herself feel something other than fear.

With each passing day, the horses kept getting better. Some days were more demanding than usual, but they were going through it. Isabella knew the vet told her that it would be a long and slow process. It felt like the road to recovery was too long. There were good days as well as bad, but things seemed to be working well.

One fine morning, Isabella, as per her routine, was in the barn before sunrise; after looking after the rest of the horses, she went to Melinda's horse. She checked on him as he had not eaten anything since the day before. He was weak and dull again, and his eyes felt defeated. Isabella's heart started to sink. She sat beside him, patting him on his shoulder. She just couldn't let him go like that.

"You're not done yet. You hear me? "You have to stay," she whispered into his ears.

But the horse didn't move a bit, which panicked Isabella. She stood up, facing toward the wall with deep sorrow; her eyes were filled with tears. She felt extremely hopeless. This was not how it was supposed to end; he should have been stronger by now. Why is this happening? An instant feeling of deep regret grew in Isabella's heart, eating her from within.

But then something moved; God listened to Isabella's prayers, and the horse moved. Isabella froze; her heart skipped a beat. She slowly turned away to find out that it was her beloved horse. Their eyes locked with each other for a moment, and a little spark of recognition hit. It wasn't a lot, but it gave Isabella a sense of relief. Her heart swelled up, and tears of joy began to fall from her eyes. Her fear didn't go away, but in that moment, it didn't matter. The only thing to be happy was that there was still hope and a little energy left in him to fight through.

Soon, the other horses were showing progress. They were healing, getting better, and their coats were shining, but Melinda's horse was still far behind on his journey of recovery. His eyes were not hollow anymore, and his appetite had somewhat returned, but still it was a long way to full recovery.

Long… exhausting… and tiring… the road to recovery is not the easiest—not only for the ones suffering but also for those caring for them, spending every living moment, praying and hoping for a miracle.

Isabella had to be patient with the progress. Isabella knew only one thing: no matter what happens, she would not leave his beloved horses' side.

*Not now, not ever.*

# XI

# A Healing Bond

The air was crisp that morning, and the soft scent of hay filled the air as Isabella walked toward the barn. The surroundings were quiet as if everything had held its breath. Inside the stable, the horses made a quiet motion, but one stall reflected something that bothered Isabella. It was Huckleberry's.

The moment Isabella saw him, she knew something was wrong. His head hung low, and his demeanor, exhausted. He looked at Isabella with his eyes saying that he was just not okay. He needed help. Isabella's heart clenched.

"Not you, too," she whispered, stepping closer to Huckleberry.

She had taken care of many horses, but Huckleberry and Isabella connected with each other in a very different way. He was close to her heart. He wasn't just another horse; he was hers in a way Isabella couldn't yet explain.

Isabella had been noticing for a few days that Huckleberry was being lethargic. His bright eyes were dull, and his appetite was diminishing. Worried, Isabella called Dr. James, the veterinarian, After the thorough examination of Huckleberry, Dr. James shared the devastating news— throat tumor.

Isabella felt like her world had come crashing down. The word 'tumor' was haunting her, but she refused to surrender before Huckleberry's illness.

"Whatever it takes, we'll fight with it," she told Dr. James, her voice determined.

Huckleberry's illness brought a side of Isabella she had not known existed. She spent hours sitting beside his stall, caressing his neck and whispering words of encouragement. Isabella's love for him grew stronger with each passing day. As his illness progressed, Isabella not only cared for him physically but also poured her heart into the bond they both shared. It was not only about fulfilling his needs—it was about being there for him. Huckleberry had a way to sense it when she used to get upset. He would nuzzle at her or keep his head on her shoulder; it was his way of reassuring Isabella that she wasn't alone. The love between them was enough for them to carry through the most challenging times in their lives.

"You're my Huckleberry," she'd say with a smile, borrowing a line from the movie Tombstone. It became her slogan, a declaration of a beautiful bond they both shared.

The once carefree, energetic woman who had spent her days running around the barn with her horses was now sinking into a quiet intensity. What surprised Isabella the most was Huckleberry's reaction to her sadness. It was as if he could always sense whenever she got upset. Even when she tried to hide her emotions, Huckleberry would just know it. On days like that, he would lower his head to her level, placing it on her shoulder as if to say,

*I am here for you, too.*

It was like he knew that as much as he needed her, Isabella needed Huckleberry, too. The act of gently nuzzling his head at her back or placing his head on her shoulder became Isabella's support on the days when she felt devastated. With every moment spent together, their bond strengthened. It was a bond that Isabella hadn't experienced before; she just loved him so much!

Isabella dwelled on the research treatments for Huckleberry's illness. She consulted with a specialist, Dr. Ali, and he suggested corticosteroids for the reduction of the swelling around his throat. Moreover, he suggested a diet plan that would support Huckleberry's immune system. Isabella discussed having surgery for the removal of the tumor, but Dr. Ali denied it after examining Huckleberry's overall condition.

She then tried veterinary herbalist, Dr. Thomas for Huckleberry's illness. He recommended a blend of herbal medicines, like turmeric and ashwagandha to boost his immune system. She spent sleepless nights trying herbal medications for him, massaging his neck to ease his discomfort.

Every day that passed led to further deterioration of his health; she could now see his ribs more clearly. His once-strong body was thinning, yet he stood firm and tried to snack on his food. Small victories like these kept Isabella strong. Her determination never wavered. Huckleberry grew weaker and thinner, but his zest remained unbroken.

What Isabella admired the most about Huckleberry was his resilience. Even in the face of constant discomfort, he refused to let go of his energy. He radiated a sense of peace and self-acceptance as if he had already accepted his fate, that, too, with grace. This quiet acceptance was unsettling for Isabella. Huckleberry's calmness used to bother Isabella sometimes, but his patience taught her that you can't fight with destiny.

What's yet to happen will happen anyway, so we must accept it wholeheartedly instead of crying about the situation.

As Huckleberry's condition worsened, Isabella found herself on an unexpected spiritual journey. By taking care of him, she confronted her own vulnerabilities and fears. She learned to find hope even in the most difficult moments and to focus on the small victories—a day when Huckleberry eats a full meal or when his eyes sparkle with joy again.

Isabella was amazed by his calm acceptance. While suffering with immense pain, how could he remain so peaceful? But Huckleberry's strength gave her a sense of clarity she had long been searching for. She began to understand that resilience isn't about fighting for your fate but surrendering to the present moment. It taught her the lesson of hope, optimism, and living in the moment. It was as if he showed her how to focus on the present and be thankful for whatever you have. He taught her how to embrace one's fears and to trust that there is a unknown force that is guiding them both.

More than anything, Huckleberry taught Isabella to live in the moment. Each day with him was a gift for her, a reminder to cherish the time they had left to spend together rather than focusing on the unavoidable. His presence healed her in ways she hadn't anticipated. He taught Isabella the art of letting things go in a way that would nourish, rather than rupture, one's soul.

"It's like God sent him to me," she expressed to Melinda on call. "I feel like I am meant to be his voice, to fight for him when he can't."

Melinda nodded with her damp eyes, "Maybe he's fighting for you, too."

Despite Isabella's uncountable efforts, the tumor kept on growing. Huckleberry's health was declining, and there was nothing she could do to stop it. He was in immense pain; Isabella knew that the time was nearing when she'd have to make an impossible decision. The thought of losing Huckleberry had been haunting Isabella for days, but she could not bear to see him suffer from pain.

In Huckleberry's last days, their bond grew stronger. Isabella used to spend hours with him, her forehead resting against his as she whispered prayers and promises in his ear. But Huckleberry, as always, seemed to understand. He would nuzzle at her gently as if he wanted to tell Isabella that everything was going to be okay if she let go of things.

On a cool fall morning, with the sun pouring golden light across the barn, Isabella sat beside Huckleberry, her heart heavy with uncertainty. Though his health was declining, he kept his head on her shoulder, offering the comfort that he always gave. In those moments, Isabella softly whispered in his ears, her voice steady despite the tears rolling down her cheeks.

"You're my Huckleberry," she mumbled in his ears while her fingers gently ran through his crests. The words carried a promise of unwavering love and presence.

Huckleberry's breath was painful, and Isabella knew that the road ahead would not be easy. But as she sat with him, she felt a renewed sense of determination. This wasn't the end, not yet. She still had time to cherish, fight, and hope. As she left the barn that morning, she paused to look back. Huckleberry lifted his head slightly, his eyes following her with a look that said,

*I am still here.*

Isabella wiped her tears and smiled softly. The journey was a bit far from over, and she was not giving up on him. Whatever lay ahead, she would face it together with her steadfast companion.

# XII

# Saying Goodbye

"Is this what they mean when they say the hardest choices are the right ones?" Isabella murmured to herself as her voice broke the silence of the barn. As she sat outside Huckleberry's stall, the test results clutched tightly in her hand. The words on the page looked like a bitter joke: A deadly tumor no viable treatment. Isabella tried reading it repeatedly, but sadly, the meaning didn't change.

Inside, Huckleberry moved slightly. His weakened body was still managing a silent strength that broke her heart. Isabella leaned her head against the wooden wall, trying to gain the strength to face Huckleberry. However, Isabella had made difficult decisions regarding rescues, recoveries, and even said tough goodbyes. But this? This felt different. It was something new, something she wasn't ready for.

She let out a deep breath and stepped into Huckleberry's stall. The smell was familiar: mixed hay and the bittersweet smell of medicine. Huckleberry turned his head toward her, his large, soulful eyes meeting hers. Those eyes—so full of trust and quiet understanding—broke down the last of her resolve.

"Hey, buddy," she said softly, her voice shaking.

She reached out to him and gently ran her hand along Huckleberry's neck, her fingers running through his thinning coat.

"You've always known, haven't you? You've known what I couldn't admit to myself."

Huckleberry nuzzled her gently, the way he always did when she was upset. Although his sweet gesture was small yet full of love, it undid her. She sank to her knees in the straw, wrapping her arms around his neck and burying her face in his mane.

"I'm so sorry," she whispered through tears. "I wish I could fix this. I wish I could make it all go away."

The test results were an emotional hit for Isabella, leaving her devastated. The tumor Huckleberry carried was not just dangerous—it was deadly. The infection had spread beyond what any medication could reach. And there was no cure, no treatment that could spare him more suffering. Isabella knew what had to be done, but knowing didn't make it any easier.

Isabella spent days researching medications, consulting specialists, and even considering unconventional treatments, but she somewhere knew in her heart that Huckleberry was not healthy enough to endure any more pain. She was circled back to the same grim conclusion of letting him return to his owner.

After pulling herself together, Isabella courageously called Huckleberry's owner; the sun was about to set, casting long shadows across the barn's floor. She stared at the phone for a long time, her fingers hovering over the screen. Finally, she pressed the button.

The owner picked up on the second ring. "Hello?"

Isabella cleared her throat, struggling to steady her voice. "Hi, it's Isabella. I… I have the test results."

"Oh?" There was a hopeful lilt in the woman's voice, one that made Isabella's chest tighten.

"It's not good news," Isabella said, her words slow and deliberate. "Huckleberry has a severe, untreatable tumor. There's nothing we can do to save him without causing more pain. I've been fighting this in my head all day, but I know we have to let him go. It's the only humane option."

The line went silent. Then, a shaky voice replied, "I didn't realize it was this serious. Are you sure there's nothing else?"

"If there were, I'd be doing it," Isabella said gently. "I wish I had better news. I truly do. But this is about his comfort now, not ours."

The owner let out a long, shuddering sigh. "I trust you to do what's best. Thank you for being there for him."

When the call ended, Isabella sat quietly for a long time. The decision was made, but it didn't feel like relief. It felt like a heavy, hollow ache in her chest. She turned her eyes toward Huckleberry, who stood calmly in his stall as if he were carrying the weight of the decision with her.

In the evening, Isabella brought a soft blanket and a handful of Huckleberry's favorite treats into the barn. She didn't know how much time they had left together, but she was determined to make every moment count.

As she draped the blanket over his back, she ran her hands softly on his coat, feeling his warmth.

"I never imagined this would be how it would end," she whispered sadly into his ear. "You've been so strong, Huckleberry. I don't know how you've done it, but you taught me so much. I wish I could do more for you."

Her voice trembles. "I just want to tell you that I am extremely grateful for you and everything you have given me."

He turned his head slightly, his ears flicking as if he were listening. Isabella smiled faintly.

"It suits you; you know. You've got this fighting spirit, so strong and determined. But you're also so gentle that only a few people see it. That's who you are. Strong, tender, and one of a kind."

Huckleberry nickered softly, the sound almost reassuring. Isabella laughed through her tears.

"That's it, isn't it? You're my Huckleberry."

The phrase had always been a private declaration of their bond. Saying it now felt like sealing a promise to honor their time together and the lessons he had taught her.

As night fell, Isabella sat with Huckleberry, gently rubbing her hands on his body and whispering stories about the other horses she had cared for. She told him how grateful she was for him and how much he had taught her about resilience and love.

"You've changed me, you know," she said quietly. "You've taught me to live in the moment. To stop worrying about what's next and just… be here. Right now."

Huckleberry stood quietly, his head resting against her shoulder. It was his way of offering comfort, even in his deteriorating state.

When she considered the message his story could carry to others, Isabella felt a glimmer of hope, which appeared in her sorrow. Huckleberry's journey was a testament to acceptance—to finding peace in the face of difficulties and embracing the present moment, no matter how temporary.

She thought back to the other horses she had helped, and a sense of purpose began to take root in her grief. These animals came to her because they knew she would do right by them when they are suffering, even when the choices were impossibly hard. For that purpose, she found some relief.

When the time finally came, Isabella held Huckleberry close, her hands trembling as she stroked his neck. "Thank you," she whispered, her voice thick with emotion. "Thank you for trusting me, teaching me, and being exactly who you are."

With a heavy heart, Isabella led Huckleberry to the waiting Veterinarian. Each step felt like a farewell. She was hiding her emotions, which were spinning between gratitude and sorrow. As she walked through the paddocks memories of their journey together filled her mind. Isabella recalled countless beautiful times they had spent together, how he began to trust humans again, and showed unyielding strength even in his weakest moments. Even though their time together had been short, it had been more meaningful than she could have imagined.

When they reached the familiar medical paddock where the Doctor was waiting, she unlatched the fence  and walked alongside him as he made his way back into the stable. Isabella paused, watching him take the first few steps. There was a calmness to him now, an acceptance of how he moved as if he understood that this was how it was meant to be.

Turning to give him one last look, Isabella whispered, "You'll always be my Huckleberry."

The emotional weight of the past few days lingered in her chest, but there was something else—peace, though faint, was slowly settling in. Isabella knew that Huckleberry had come into her life for a reason. He had shown her the true meaning of resilience and the importance of living in the moment, accepting what life brought without trying to control every part of it.

Later that evening, after she had settled into her small apartment, Isabella dialed Melinda's number. She needed someone to share the burden with, someone who could understand the heaviness in her heart.

"Mel, I just sent him to the veterinarian" Isabella's voice cracked as she spoke into the phone. "Huckleberry… I had to let him go."

Melinda said reassuringly, "You did the right thing, Isabella. You gave him peace when no one else could."

Isabella paused, letting the words sink in. "I hope you're right. It feels so empty right now, but I know… I know it was the only way."

"I'm here for you," Melinda reassured her, the warmth in her voice a small comfort across the miles. "You gave him more than anyone else could have. You gave him love and care, and freedom from pain, and in the end, that's what mattered the most."

Isabella nodded to herself, even though she knew Melinda couldn't see her. "Thanks, Mel. I just wish… I could have done more."

"Sometimes the greatest gift we can give is letting go when it's time," Melinda said, her words gentle but wise.

Isabella felt a sense of peace she hadn't realized she needed. With a quiet sigh, she ended the call, knowing that Huckleberry's spirit—his fighting strength and gentle soul—would stay with her forever.

# XIII

# Forever Grateful

"Do you ever feel like some souls find us exactly the moment we need them?"

Isabella asked, her voice soft, almost yearning, as she leaned back on her porch swing. The sun went down on the horizon, painting the sky in soft oranges and purples. Melinda's laughter came through the phone, warm and familiar.

"You're asking me that? You know I do. Why, though? Thinking about Huckleberry again?"

"Not just thinking about him," Isabella admitted. "I still feel him, Mel. Every time I step into the barn or even sit here like this, I feel like he's still with me, nudging on my shoulder. Ah! I can't explain it in words. I feel his presence here. I miss him."

"You don't have to," Melinda said gently. "That's the magic of it, isn't it? Some bonds don't fade just because time or space separates you."

Isabella smiled with a bittersweet ache sparking in her chest. "He taught me more in my short time with him than I've learned in years of working with horses. It wasn't just about care or trust but something deeper. He showed me how to forgive, live in the moment, and find peace even when everything feels impossible."

"You know," Melinda replied after a pause, "you've always had a way of seeing what others can't, especially with animals. But it sounds like he saw you, too. Maybe that's why he found you."

As the call ended and Isabella sat in the quiet of her home, she let her thoughts move to Huckleberry again. The barn felt emptier without him, but his presence stayed in the details: the worn harness hanging on the wall, the faint scent of hay that seemed to cling to her clothes.

As much as his parting away broke Isabella's heart, she couldn't help but smile at the memories they had created together. When she thought about their time together, one memory stood out—a moment that captured the essence of Huckleberry and the ways he used to show his love for Isabella.

One day, it was a chilly evening, and Isabella was disturbed by several setbacks. As she leaned against the stall door, tears poured down from her eyes, trying to suppress the weight of her frustration. Despite the fact that Huckleberry was going through a rough patch in his life, he somehow sensed it right that Isabella was in sorrow. He moved closer to her and rested his head softly on her shoulder. It wasn't just a gesture; it was a message. I'm here. You're not alone.

"That's who he was," Isabella whispered, a tear sliding down her cheek. "Even when he was suffering, he found a way to comfort me. How could I ever repay that kind of love?"

Huckleberry had taught her more in their brief time together than she had learned in years of working with horses. Forgiveness, she realized, was one of his greatest lessons.

"Holding onto anger or pain… it only steals the moments you have," Isabella wrote in her journal one evening. "It doesn't fix anything. It doesn't heal. All it does is take away the time you could have spent loving, learning, and living."

She thought about the moments she had wasted in her own life—grudges held, fears she clung to, regrets that had kept her from moving forward. Huckleberry had shown her that life was too precious for that weight.

Isabella knew precisely what she would say if she could speak to him again.

"Thank you," she murmured to the empty room as if he could somehow hear her. "Thank you for sharing your time with me, reaching out to me, and offering life's most precious lessons. You gave me more than I ever gave you, and I'll never forget that."

She had the idea to write a book in the quiet hours after Huckleberry had left. It wasn't just about preserving his memory but about sharing his story with the world.

"Horses like Huckleberry… they're more than just animals," Isabella told Melinda during one of their late-night calls.

"They understand us in ways we don't even understand ourselves. They see our pain, joy, and flaws and love us anyway."

Melinda's voice was warm on the other end. "And you're the perfect person to tell that story. You've always seen them for who they are. This book… it's going to change people, Isabella."

Isabella smiled, feeling a sense of purpose she hadn't felt in weeks. "I hope so," she said softly. "If even one person understands how special they are—how much they give without asking for anything in return—it'll be worth it."

As Isabella poured her heart into the pages of the book, she found herself revisiting every moment she had shared with Huckleberry. She expressed her gratitude for his quiet strength and gentle spirit and how he had transformed her life in ways she hadn't thought possible.

Huckleberry's legacy was alive, reaching people in ways she had only hoped it would.

As she sat on her couch one evening, looking at the stars, Isabella felt a deep sense of peace, as if Huckleberry had somehow once again comforted her. Although her time with Huckleberry had been brief, it had changed her forever. He had taught her to forgive, love, and live fully in the present.

"I'll always be grateful for you," she whispered to the night sky. "Always."

And in the quiet that followed, she felt him there—his spirit lingering in the lessons he had left behind, the love he had given, and the lives he had touched.

The time she spent with Huckleberry shaped her life in ways she never could have imagined. Isabella gave him her heart, and in return, he gave her far more valuable lessons—lessons of forgiveness, hope, and courage to live fully in the present. His quiet strength had taught her the power of vulnerability and how much it could change the course of a life. Huckleberry had shown her, in the most profound way, that holding onto pain or displeasure only takes away the joy of the present moment. He had lived in the moment with such grace and love, and that was something Isabella would carry with her forever.

Her heart swelled with deep and unshakeable gratitude, and a quiet peace settled within her. Writing this book and sharing Huckleberry's story wasn't just about honoring him—it was about honoring the lessons he had imparted. He had shown her that hope wasn't a distant dream but something alive in the present, in each moment, no matter how fleeting. Although his time spent with Isabella had been brief yet, he had impacted her in ways that would last forever.

And even though their time together had ended, his influence on her life would remain a guiding light. She would carry it with her always—forever grateful for the horse who had shown her how to live, how to forgive, and most of all, how to love without reservation.

"Goodbye, Huckleberry," she whispered softly, her eyes glistening with unshed tears. "Thank you for everything. I will always be grateful."

# XIV

# Epilogue



*"The greatness of a nation and its moral progress can be judged by the way its animals are treated."*

— Mahatma Gandhi.

The barn was quiet except for the soft rustle of hay and the occasional soft neighing of the horses. Isabella walked past the stalls, patting a nose here, scratching behind an ear there, whispering soft words of encouragement. This was her happy place—a place where she felt most at peace.

Every corner of this barn reminded her of Huckleberry. His story had changed her life and guided her work. Now, everything she did—therapy sessions, workshops, conversations—was shaped by what he had taught her.

Huckleberry had come into her life at a time when she didn't even know she needed him. He had shown her how to forgive, how to live in the moment, and how to find peace even during life's most challenging moments. His memory was alive in every horse she cared for, every person she helped, and every story she shared.

One of her favorite things to do now was to introduce people to the healing power of horses. Horses had now become an integral part of her psychotherapy sessions, and the results were nothing short of magical.

"Horses have a way of knowing what you're feeling even when you don't," she often explained to her clients. "They don't judge, and they don't rush you. They just stand there with you, giving you the space to feel whatever you need to feel."

Time and time again, Isabella watched as her clients opened up in the presence of the horses. People who had spent years bottling up their emotions suddenly found themselves talking freely, their hands resting gently on a horse's neck. The horses didn't say a word, but their presence made all the difference.

It wasn't just her clients who were affected. Isabella herself had changed. The journey with Huckleberry and the other rescued horses had given her a sense of purpose she'd never felt before.

"I feel like I'm their voice now," she told Melinda one evening as they were on a call. "Every horse that's been mistreated or misunderstood; I'm speaking for them. I'm showing the world how special they are."

Melinda smiled. "You've always had a way with them, Isabella. But now, you're doing something so much bigger. You're making a difference for the horses and for the people who get to experience their magic."

Isabella had started sharing Huckleberry's story with anyone who would listen. She spoke at schools, community centers, and equestrian events, raising awareness about neglected and abused horses.

"At first, people don't believe me when I tell them how the horses came into my life," she said during one of her talks. "They think it's just a coincidence. But it's not. It's something bigger—what I call quantum entanglement. These horses were meant to find me, and I was meant to share their story."

She taught others how to care for their horses properly, showing them that building a bond was about more than just feeding and grooming. It was about trust, understanding, and mutual respect.

"Horses have been with us for thousands of years," she often said. "They've gone to war with us, carried our loads,  explored new lands by our side, plough our field for food, been our companions, and our transportation. They've given us everything, and all they ask for in return is kindness. That's the least we owe them."

Whenever the challenges of her work felt overwhelming, Isabella reminded herself why she was doing it. It wasn't just about helping the horses— it was about helping people, too.

"Horses are mankind's partners," she said to one of her clients during a session. "They've been with us through thick and thin. When you build a connection with a horse, you're not just training them but building a relationship with them. And that can change your life." Her eyes softened with the memory of Huckleberry.

As the session ended, Isabella, on her way home, saw the kids interacting with their horses. She saw their tentative strokes, smiles, and moments of connection formed. This reminded her of the times she had with Huckleberry, a horse who needed healing but with so much love to give.

Looking back on everything she'd been through; Isabella felt a deep sense of gratitude. Huckleberry had brought purpose to her life in a way she never could have imagined.

"Huckleberry gave me so much more than I gave him," she reflected one evening, standing by the paddock as the sun dipped below the horizon. "He taught me how to forgive, how to hope, and how to truly live. Because of him, I know what it means to connect with people, with animals, and with life itself."

Her message to the world was clear and simple:

"Horses are more than just animals. They understand us in ways we can't even explain. They read our energy and our body language, and they respond with love and loyalty. They deserve to be treated with respect, care, and compassion."

Isabella paused as if imagining Huckleberry standing beside her, his soulful eyes meeting hers. She continued with her soft but firm voice, "Horses have stood by humanity for centuries—not just as workers but as companions. They've carried our burdens, shared our victories, and comforted us in our sorrows. Yet, so many people neglect, abandon, and misunderstand them. This isn't just unfair; it's heartbreaking."

For Isabella, this wasn't just a belief, it was a way of life. She lived by what she preached by showing people how to treat horses with care and build a meaningful bond with them. These actions made people more empathic and kinder toward horses. Isabella used to conduct meetings with several horse owners to teach them how to tack horses and communicate with them on a deeper level.

"It's not about controlling them," she explained. "It's about partnership. Horses don't need to be dominated but to be understood. That's when the real magic happens."

Huckleberry's story wasn't just about the past; it was about the future; it was about the lives he would touch, the lessons he would pass on, and the bond between humans and horses that would continue to grow.

"Huckleberry," she whispered to herself, her voice filled with emotion. Thank you for everything. You changed my life, and I'll spend the rest of it making sure your story and legacy live on."

While looking at the night sky, she turned and headed back to the barn, her heart full of hope and gratitude. Huckleberry's legacy would live on in her work, in the people she touched, and in the horses, whose lives she continued to save. As long as she had breath in her lungs, she would carry his story forward, forever grateful for the horse who gave her life a purpose.

www.ingramcontent.com/pod-product-compliance
Lightning Source LLC
Chambersburg PA
CBHW051908250726
48659CB00002B/541